Photoshop Box Set

Table of Contents

3

Disclaimer

Introduction

Photoshop was launched in February of 1990 and its launch totally changed the way digital images were handled. It caused a stir in the global creative community and made it really easy for everyone to edit images without the need to buy expensive equipment. The revolution started by Photoshop in 1990 is still alive today. Despite other software in the market like Paint.net, Photoshop still provides the best flexibility and user interface. That is why even after facing competition for more than 22 years,

Adobe Photoshop is still the global standard for every company to edit and build images.

Over the years, Adobe has added extra features to Photoshop, making it more complex for beginners to learn Photoshop from start to finish. This book provides a path for beginners to follow with which they can not only start using Photoshop today but will also be able to build their basic foundation in Photoshop so that they don't face any difficulty in learning the complete Photoshop later.

In this book, you will learn the tools, panels and basics of Photoshop. By reading this book, you will find that there is more than one way of doing the same task. You are correct. Photoshop is a vast software and each task can be completed in a number of ways. For beginners, I recommend finding a method that they like and just stick to it. Don't confuse yourself by trying to implement every single available method. So let the learning begin.

Different Version of Photoshop

If you ask a Photoshop expert, or even if you just do a Google search, you will see that there are two names which keep coming up when you search for Photoshop. These are, Adobe Photoshop CS and Adobe Photoshop CC. Most beginners are confused between the two versions. That's why I want to clear the difference in CS and CC version of Photoshop before moving on in this book. CS in Adobe Photoshop stands for Creative Suite, while CC stands for Creative Cloud.

A Creative Suite is a standard desktop Photoshop Application like other apps that you have on your desktop. A major release is made by Adobe every two years or so, and the user needed to pay once in order to get that release. Each release used to be packed with updates and new features. However, Adobe has now moved from CS to CC.

A Photoshop Creative Cloud is also a desktop application that you download and install on your computer. However, it is a bit different from the CS version. Creative Cloud is continuously updated by Adobe as its developers work on bug fixes and releasing new features. All these updates are downloaded automatically to the user's computer by Adobe manager. In order to use the creative cloud, a user has to subscribe to a monthly subscription of the software, just like they subscribe to any monthly magazine. The CC version has more features than CS version (more than 15 new features were added in 2013 and still counting).

Both versions work the same and that's why it does not matter which Photoshop version you have right now. This book will assist you for both versions.

Getting Started with Photoshop

Before you start using Adobe Photoshop for editing images, you first need to make yourself comfortable with the Photoshop workspace. A workspace is an area on your screen where you work in Photoshop. Photoshop is infinitely customizable and modular in its layout. When you open Photoshop for the first time, you will see all the tools listed on the left side of the screen, while all the panels are on the right side of the screen. Besides the tools and panels, you will also see a standard menu at the top of your

screen.

Photoshop Workspace

Below is an image to give you an overview of the

workspace of the Adobe Photoshop including various

panels and a tool bar.

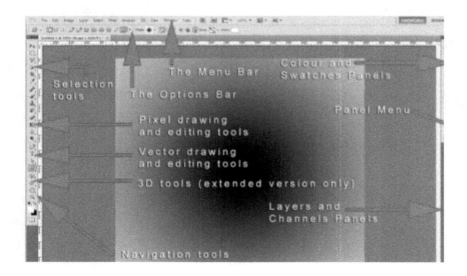

In the above image, you will see the following elements:

- The menu bar

- The options bar

- Left side tool bar including selection tools, navigation tools, pixel drawing and editing tools, 3D tools, and vector drawing and editing tools.

- Color and Swatches Panel

- Panel Menu

- Layer and channel panels followed by panel options

In both Photoshop CC and Photoshop CS, you will see these elements. The position of few elements may differ, like color swatches may appear at the bottom in Photoshop CC, unlike on the right side in Photoshop CS. But, it doesn't matter as in both of the versions, all the elements, with the exception of menu bar, are mobile. You can drag them around and place them anywhere to create your own working place. You should have all the above mentioned elements on your Photoshop screen. If you are not able to see some of the elements, then you will have to get them on screen manually. Simply go to menu bar, click Windows and select a workspace. Now you can get all the elements on your screen. Now, let's discuss each element in Photoshop.

The Tool Bar

The tool bar, also known as the tool panel, is located on the left side of the work area by default. It contains many mouse based tools that a user selects while working in Photoshop for editing and navigating purposes. In the above workspace image, I have already named the various sections of tools that are present in this tool bar. These sections are created by Photoshop itself to loosely group the tools based on their functionality. You will see that these sections are separated by a small line. The first group of tools is selection tools, which are followed by pixel editing tools, vector editing tools and navigation tools. After all the sections, you will see a color picker at the bottom of the tool bar and an icon that allows you to enter the quick mask mode for editing and creating selections. The tool bar is summed up in one image below to help you understand better.

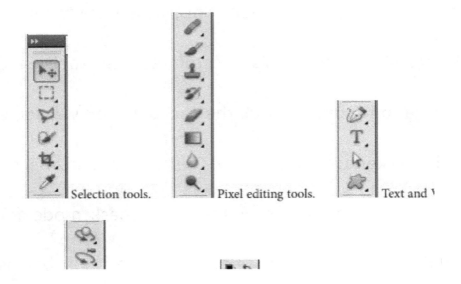

Selection tools.   Pixel editing tools.   Text and

In the above image, you will notice that most of the

tools have a small black arrow at the right bottom.

Most of the beginners ignore this arrow icon. This

icon actually means that there are more tools that

can be accessed by the user by clicking and holding

the tool. Once you do that, a list of extra tools will

appear. After the list appears, you can release the mouse and the list will remain for you to make a selection. A comprehensive example of the extra tools list is shown in the image below.

Now, let's investigate some of the common tools used by beginners in Photoshop. It is recommended that you follow this book to open these tools and try using them as you read about them for better understanding.

The Move Tool

This is the most widely used tool in Photoshop or in any other image editing software available. You can move objects around the photoshop campus using the move tool. Click any point on the canvas and drag,

The Marquee Tool

The next most widely used tool for beginners is the marquee tool. The user can select the canvas in a shape of this choice. A rectangular shape is default, but the user can change to an ellipsis shape if needed.

The Lasso Tool

This is the tool which gets all beginners excited in Photoshop. Most users start selecting with Lasso Tool even in the case where a marquee tool can be used. The lasso tool lets you choose different parts of the canvas like a lasso, in a free-form manner. You can choose a polygonal lasso or a magnetic lasso tool. The magnetic lasso automatically detects edges for you.

The Magic Wand Tool

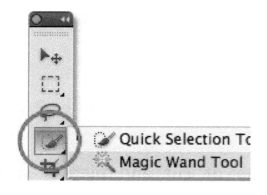

This tool makes selection and editing easy when an area of similar color is to be selected quickly. This tool can be used as an out of the box method to remove backgrounds from photos. Using this tool makes photoshop select the spot that's selected and anything around it.

The Crop Tool

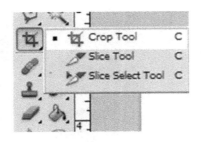

This tool is used to crop or cut and picture in Photoshop to any size that you wish.

The Eyedropper Tool

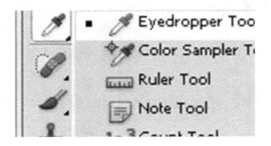

The Eyedropper lets you pick any color in your foreground or background as your selected color.

The Healing Brush Tool

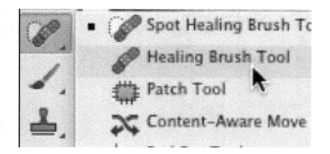

This is another famous tool for both beginners and intermediates of Photoshop. This lets you use part of the photograph to paint over another part. Photoshop will blend the surrounding areas of the picture as required.

Pencil and Paintbrush Tools

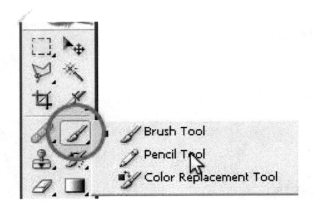

This is like being used as a pencil. It can be adjusted to various sizes and shapes.

The Eraser Tool

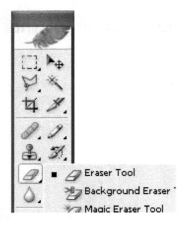

This is another tool that you must be familiar with because of the Paint application on your desktop or laptop. The eraser tool is almost identical to the paintbrush tool in Photoshop. The only difference is that it erases instead of painting a canvas.

The Paint Bucket & Gradient Tool

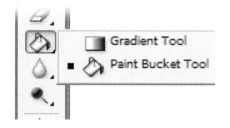

Again, the paint bucket is already known to you, but the gradient tool is a new term for you, right? I am going to explain both of them simultaneously so you will understand better. The paint bucket tool works in a similar manner to the paint application, and lets you fill it in with a certain foreground color. The gradient tool will blend the background with the foreground by creating a gradient. You can choose level and type of gradients required. These preset gradients are available in two or more colors which you can use.

The Pen Tool

Suppose that the magic wand tool was of no help in changing the image's background because the background and image were very similar in color. In such cases, using a pen tool acts as a life saver for Photoshop users. Mastering the pen tool is the most challenging part for Photoshop beginners. But believe me, once you start using it, you will love it. As this tool is really important for Photoshop users, let's learn in detail about how to use it.

To start with the Pen tool, open an image with a basic shape in Photoshop. Now, select the pen tool and click to create the edges of your shape. After completing it, you will see a little O if you hover over the first point. You can then click on that first point to close the shape. Hold ALT/OPT and click on a point to turn it from a curve to a straight line, and vice versa. It sounds really simple, doesn't it? But once you start using it, you will understand how much patience is required to master this small yet important tool.

The Text Tool

T

You must be familiar with this tool from the paint application on your desktop. However, the text tool is a little bit advanced in Photoshop. The text tool in Photoshop allows you to write in two different ways. It is really important that you understand both of these. The first way is how most people use text, by using what is called the Point text tool. You simply click on the Text Tool in the tools palette, click back on your image and start typing. The other way is to click on the Text Tool if it's not already clicked. Take the text tool and DRAG it out to make a rectangle. Now, you will be able to type in this rectangular box and all the text that you type will be constrained by this box. This is known as Paragraph text. The paragraph text can be aligned in the box to the left, right, center or justify format as per your needs. One of the advantages of having a CC over CS is that CC support offers more fonts than CS version of Photoshop.

The Shape Tool

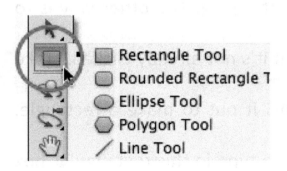

This tool makes creating simple shapes easy. With this tool, you can create vector rectangles, rounded rectangles, circles, polygons, lines, and custom shapes. These shapes are very useful when designing or when creating shape masks for photos.

Source: Lifehacker, "Learn the Basics of Photoshop in Under 25 Minutes"

The Options Bar

The options bar is another important element of the workspace. I call it the sensitive bar as it is sensitive to the tool that you select for working in Photoshop. This bar provides access to the important configuration settings for a particular tool that is active in your workspace. For example, in the image below, you can see the options bar showing various options for the move tool.

The Menu Bar

The menu bar consists of many menus and submenus which provide the user with various features of Photoshop that he can use in his work. We are going to discuss a little about all these menus to give you the basic idea of what is in each of the menus.

File Menu

This menu deals with an opening, saving a project along with exporting of it in different formats (discussed later in this book).

Edit Menu

It deals with copy, cut, and paste. In Photoshop, it's also where you transform layers and set your color spaces.

Image Menu

The image brings you canvas and image adjustments, it includes destructive effects. Options in this menu are designed to affect the image as a whole, although many adjustments are applied to only a single layer.

Layer Menu

Layers are discussed later in this book, so let's not stress about it here. For now, just understand that this menu also lets you create adjustment layers and smart objects.

Select Menu

The name itself will give you the basic idea of this menu. While the marquee and lasso tools will be your main means of selecting things, along with the pen tool once you will learn how to use it. But still, the select menu can help you refine that selection or create entirely new selections based on some criteria.

Window Menu

The window lets you hide and show certain windows and palettes. You can also arrange your Photoshop windows and palettes however you want and save them as a window preset.

There are many other menus like 3D, View which is not discussed as these are not much use for beginners in Photoshop. For now, let us just stick to the menus discussed in this book and move on to the next chapter.

Basic Operations in Photoshop

Before you start thinking about what could be the basic operations in Photoshop, let me tell you they are far more basic than you think. These are:

- Opening a file

- Saving a file

- Starting a new document

- Exporting a project

These may sound too basic and you may feel like skipping this chapter. **Don't.** At the end of this chapter you will understand there was so much that you didn't know about these operations before reading this chapter. So, let's start.

Opening a File

It is easy to open a file in Photoshop. The process is simple and the same as every other software that you use on your computer. Press Ctrl+O or go to file menu then click open and select the file that you want to open.

However, Photoshop comes with another option which is **Open As**. So, what is Open As? With this option, you will have the flexibility to open a file in a certain format in Photoshop in a totally different format. You will get a better idea with the help of image that you will see at the end of this paragraph. One useful application of this command is that you can open most of the single layer file formats in Camera Raw Document format. After opening your file in this format in Adobe Photoshop, you can easily make simple adjustments to your image without having to deal with any complex techniques in Photoshop.

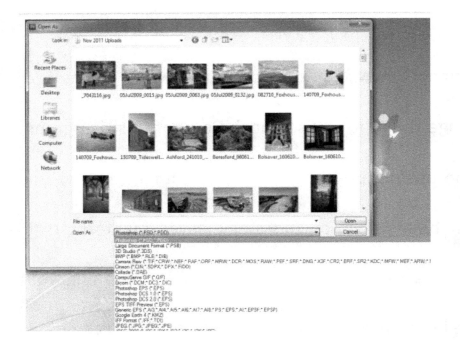

Another important term in this basic operation is

Open as Smart Object. Opening a file as a smart

object allows you to make non-destructive editing on

your opened file. This is useful when you are

planning to do extreme transformations on your

image. When you open a file as a smart object, you see it in the layers panel on the right side of the workspace with a small icon at the bottom right side of the file. From there you can turn the smart object ON and OFF for the file. Thus, it is clear that you can change a smart object file to an ordinary Photoshop file whenever you like.

Saving a File

The next basic operation of Photoshop is saving a file. You must be familiar with both the **Save** and **Save As** command from various applications on your computer like MS Office, etc. However, I will discuss

Save As in a little detail with you in this section. **Save As** works just like any other desktop application but the file formats provided in Photoshop are completely different. Below is an image to show you the vast list of file formats that Photoshop allows you to save your work in.

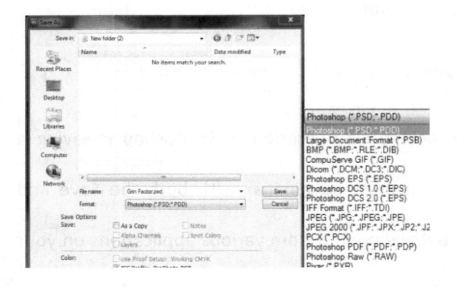

A beginner needs to understand various file formats that are used frequently for saving the work from Photoshop. These are as important as the tools that we discussed in the previous chapter. Learning about the most frequently used formats will build your basic foundation in Photoshop very quickly.

Frequent File Formats Used to Save the Work in:

PSD: It is the Photoshop's native or default file format. Whenever you save a file, the default format that Photoshop will select is PSD. It doesn't matter if the file that you were working on is a .jpg, PNG or of any other format. This format provides you the maximum flexibility in saving your work as it will retain all the layers, adjustments and effects in the manner that you applied. However, the file size for PSD format is large.

TIFF: This format is also known as TIF. It is somewhat similar to the PSD format. The main difference is that when you save your work in TIFF format, you will be able to open it in maximum image editing software as TIF format is compatible with most of the image editing software, unlike PSD. Moreover, TIFF format allows you to save your work by taking less amount of disk space than PSD due to its high compression methods.

JPG: Also known as JPEG. This is by far the most widely used image file format followed by GIF and PNG. This file format is mostly used for the images that you want to display on a screen or on the web. The file size of JPG format is smaller than PSD and TIFF. This is because most of the work is lost in the compression process thus only reflecting the final result and not saving any layers or adjustments separately like PSD and TIFF format.

PDF: You may be surprised but PDF format is really popular in Photoshop. It is very useful for displaying files across multiple applications and platforms. It provides the user with the benefit of compression and common color modes, while retaining font, vector and Photoshop editing.

Another file format which is popular in Photoshop is PNG and GIF. PNG is mostly used for making transparent images like a logo, etc., while GIF is used for making small animation images.

Creating a New Document

Creating a new document has the same command like any other computer software. Go to File and select New, or simply click Ctrl+N from your keyboard. Now, you will get a new dialogue box to set up the parameters for your new Photoshop file to start working. Most of the beginners accept the default settings or get confused in what parameters to select. Another common mistake is that each project you work on will have different sizes and resolutions for the intended purpose. Thus, using the default settings may not work sometimes. Setting up a page properly in Photoshop is really important and thus I am providing you with details of some of the most widely used settings in Photoshop for creating a new file or document.

Preset: Here, a user can select a preset for his new file. Each preset has different page sizes related to it, which can be seen in the drop-down menu below the preset. The preset size that you select will automatically set the resolution for print.

Color Mode: In color mode, RGB and CMYK are present as options. As a beginner, you should keep in mind that RGB is used for photography and web design, while CMYK is used for commercial purposes.

Bit Depth: Bit depth is another important option which is often ignored by beginners. The options in bit depth are 8 bit and 16 bit. Out of these two, the 8 bit is generally used when the user wants to do simple work unless he wants to perform some advanced image editing, which includes a lot of gradients in the design. For such cases, the 16-bit mode is used. When working with the 16-bit mode, once the user completes the work, he changes the work to an 8-bit mode as the web graphics or images are always presented in 8-bit mode.

Background Content: This option gives you the flexibility of deciding the default background color for your document.

Pixel Aspect Ratio: This setting is available in the dialogue box under advanced section. In almost all the cases, the square pixels are used. The rectangular pixels are only used when you want to display your content on a wide screen. Besides this option, the **color profile** is another important option in the advance section. I recommend you do not change anything in this section which is keeping sRGB by default. However, if you want to do some advance photographic work, then you may select Adobe RGB or Pro Photo RGB.

Most of the time when I tell beginners about color profile, I get asked the question, "What is the difference between sRGB and Adobe RGB?" For now, just keep in mind that Adobe RGB has a much wider range of colors than sRGB. Adobe RGB has 35% more color range than sRGB.

After selecting the appropriate parameters in the dialogue box, you are all set to start working in the Photoshop file. Simply click OK to get the canvas on your Photoshop screen and start working. If you are a beginner, then start with the tools that were explained earlier in the book. Use them often to get used to them.

Exporting a Project

Another important feature of Adobe Photoshop is exporting a file. However, most of the people working in Photoshop are confused in Save As and Export. This is because the work of both of these features is almost the same. With Save As, you can save the file in a different format on your computer using the Export button. However, when you save a file by using the Export function, that means that you are saving the file for some other program, whereas if you will save the file using the Save As option, it will tell Photoshop that you are saving the file for this program itself (that is the Photoshop). When you use Save As for the file, it will save the file and will let you work over that file itself in the Photoshop screen. However, if you use the Export function, then Photoshop will create a new file for the project which is not active in the Photoshop screen. Thus that file will remain unedited.

These are the basic operations in Photoshop.

Layers in Photoshop

If you thought that mastering the pen tool is the only challenge in Photoshop, then think again. Layers in Photoshop are always confusing for beginners. Beginners are known to have problems with the concept of layers and how they interact with one another in Photoshop. Layers can be grouped, duplicated, flattened, clipped, linked, renamed, reordered, blended together and hidden using the layer masks. These terms may sound overwhelming, so that's why I prefer to start from scratch on layers.

What Are Layers?

Layers are simply objects, text, images, or stacks of colors. Layers are very powerful and allow a user to edit and control the individual component without affecting any other element on the canvas in the Photoshop. The arrangement of layers plays an important role in creating images or scenes in Photoshop. Let's discuss the layers further with the help of an example.

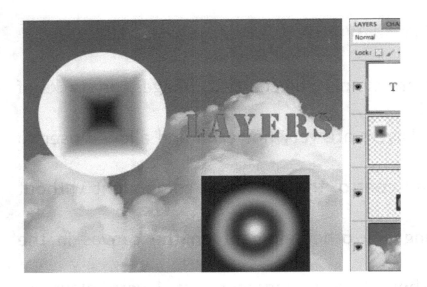

In the above image, it is clear that all the layers that

are present in a Photoshop project can be seen in the

layer panel located at the bottom right side of the

screen. In the image above, you can see that there is

a total of 5 layers, namely the background layer, the

layer with the image of the sky, the layer with the

image of a square, the layer with the image of a circle and at last, the layer with text. The layers are placed based on their arrangement in the layer panel from bottom to top. As you can see the bottom layer is the background layer, which is just below the sky layer. That is why the sky layer is covering the white background layer in the image above. The square layer is above the sky layer and has a transparent background. That is why, the square is placed over the sky in the canvas and due to the transparent background, no extra white spaces are added around the corner. The circle layer is placed above the square layer in the canvas in the same manner. The top most layer is the text layer, which is a special kind of layer. The text layer always has a white background in the layer panel. However, on canvas, the text layer always has a transparent background.

Moving Layers in Photoshop

Did you see how much your project is affected by the arrangements of the layer in the layer panel in your Photoshop? However, let's say that you want to place a square layer above the circle layer. You can do that by simply moving the layers. Moving layers in the layer panel is really easy. All you have to do is select the layers to move and then drag them up or down to the place where you want them to be in the layer panel.

Selecting the layers

When you want to select a single layer, you can do so by just clicking the layer in the layer menu. Once the layer is highlighted, then you can move it by dragging it. However, if you want to move a lot of adjacent layers, then, you can select them by clicking the first adjacent layer, then holding the shift key and clicking the last adjacent layer. After you do so, all the layers in between the first and last layer that you selected will be highlighted. Now you can move them by dragging. If you want to select multiple non-adjacent layers, then you can do so by clicking one layer, then holding the Ctrl key and clicking all the other images that you want to select. Later you can move them by dragging as usual.

Aligning the layers

When you move the layers by selecting them, they will still maintain their relative position. If you want to change the position of layers with respect to one another, then you can use the align tool. Aligning the layers is done with the help of the options bar of the layers. Let's have a look at the option bar first.

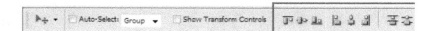

The icons in the red box in the image above are the options to align the layers. After selecting the layers just click the aligning option that you want to use to align the layers to one another. Below is an image explaining the meaning of various aligning options available for layers.

Align top edges

Align vertical centers

Align bottom edges

Align left edges

Align horizontal center:

Align right edges

Distribute top edges

Distribute vertical cente

Distribute bottom edge:

Distribute left edge:

Adjustments in Layers

Opacity

The manner in which one layer may interact with

other layers in Photoshop can be edited easily in a

number of ways to suit the needs of the user. One

such adjustment between layers is Opacity. Let's first

have a look at the options that you have in the layer

panel for the select layer.

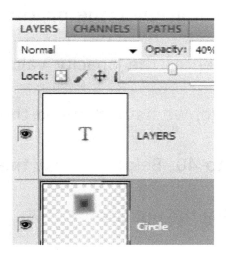

You will see two options. One of them is named

opacity and is provided with a slider. By default, the

opacity of every layer in Photoshop is 100%, but you

can edit it easily by changing the value on the slider

in the opacity option in the layer panel. Moving towards the left of the slider will reduce the opacity of the image (or layer containing that image) and moving towards the right will increase the opacity. Alternatively, you can just enter the opacity value manually. In the above image, we have changed the opacity of the circle layer to 40. Below is what the circle looks like after changing the opacity.

Blending the Layers

In the layer panel, just before the Opacity option, there is a drop-down, which has a value as 'Normal'. This drop-down is to assign a blend mode to the layers. Blend mode allows one layer to affect layers underlying it in a number of ways. You can select the

blend mode for your layers using the drop-down and

then by selecting an appropriate option.

Naming the layers

Layers by default are named as 'layer1', 'layer2', etc.,

by Photoshop. Thus, it is really easy for a user to lose

track of his work as he will not be able to remember

what layer has what components in it. Naming the

layers makes it really easy for a user to keep track of

his work. In the previous screenshots, you must have

seen that all the layers were named based on the

component that they contained (sky, circle, etc.). To

rename a layer, simply double-click the layer name in the layer panel and then type a new name.

Shape & Text Layers

Shape layers are created in the Photoshop automatically when you use the shape tool to draw shapes in your project. Similarly, the text layers are created automatically when you use the text tool in your project. When you create a shape using the shape tool, the following option comes up on the option bar.

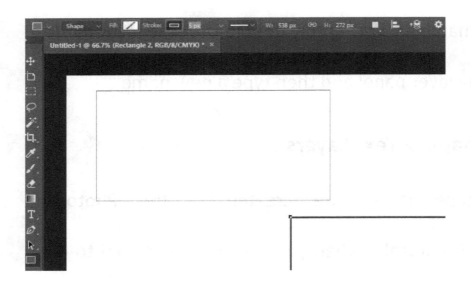

I have created two rectangles to help you understand

the necessary options from the option menu. In the

option menu, you will see **Fill** and **Stroke, W** and **H.**

You can draw a rectangle by clicking and dragging on

the canvas, and can adjust its width and height with

the help of **W** and **H** respectively. The **Fill** command

will help you fill the shape that you created with a

78

color and the **Stroke** command will help you make a shape with varying width of the outline. For example, in the image above, I have created one rectangle with 1px of stroke (the upper one) and one rectangle with 5px of strokes (the bottom one). You can simply enter the stroke value that you want. Next to the stroke value is a line drop-down available. From this drop-down, you can select different kinds of lines for your shape, like a solid line, dashed line, dotted line, etc.

Working with Images in Photoshop

Working on images to edit and modify them is the main reason why most people start using Photoshop. What you learned in this book until now must have familiarized you with Photoshop and various tools. However, I kept certain tools isolated until now so that I can explain them in this chapter. After reading and following this chapter, you will be able to edit images easily. But, first things first, let's start by discussing the tools.

Navigation & Zooming

If you would have paid enough attention in the previous chapters of the book, then you must have noticed that nowhere did I talk about any of the navigation menus. If you noticed this then you are a quick learner, if not then don't worry, it happens with many beginners.

The Zoom Tool

The zoom tool allows you to zoom in and zoom out of your canvas in Photoshop. With this tool, there are two ways to zoom in. One is by selecting the zoom tool and clicking on the desired portion of the image to zoom in predefined increments. The second

is to select the zoom tool and then drag on the image

to define the particular area that you want to zoom

in on. Now, let's take a look at the option panel for

the zoom tool. If you don't remember the option

panel, then I advise you to go back to Chapter 3 and

review it.

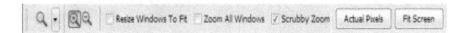

The magnifying glass with + on it indicates the zoom

in option while the magnifying glass with a − icon on

it indicates the zoom out option. You can zoom out

of the image by clicking on this icon.

If you look at the above image closely, then you will see that an option named **scrubby zoom.** This option is checked by default in Photoshop. If it isn't, then I recommend you check it manually. Scrubby zoom allows you to quickly zoom in and zoom out of your image by clicking and dragging. If you want to zoom in, then click on the image and drag to the right side of the screen. Similarly, if you want to zoom out, you can do so by clicking and dragging towards the left of the screen.

Actual Pixels in the option bar will show you the image at 100% magnification. **Fit Screen,** as the name indicates will fit the current image to your workspace screen respecting the panels and the toolbars. **Fill Screen** will zoom in and fill all your screens with the image irrespective of the panels and toolbars on your screen. **Print Size** will show you the actual printing size of the project based on the document settings that you selected while creating a new document.

The Hand Tool (Pan Tool)

After you zoom into your image, you can use the hand tool for moving the image around. Just select the tool from the navigation section and then go back to your image. Click and drag to move around in the image. If you are working on your project and don't want to change the tool, then you can just press the spacebar button on your keyboard to activate the hand tool. Your original tool will be selected automatically by Photoshop as soon as you release the spacebar button on your keyboard.

The Navigator

When you zoom into your image and move around, it is really easy to lose yourself. In this case, you can either zoom out and check your position, or simply access the navigator in Photoshop. When you turn the navigator ON, a red box will appear in the navigator dialogue over your image which will tell you about your current position in the image. Navigation can also be undertaken by dragging this red square to a new position on the image.

Navigation and Zooming plays an important role when you are editing images. That's why I kept this part for this chapter of the book. Now, let's move on and do some image editing in Photoshop.

Basic Adjustments for Images in Photoshop

In this section, I am going to tell you how to edit the whole image to adjust its size, and how to apply adjustments to the image, for example, color, brightness, etc. There are two ways to apply adjustments in Photoshop. The first is to go to the Image menu in the Menu bar and then going to Adjustments. In the Adjustment submenu, you will see a total of 22 adjustments or edits available. Any adjustment that you make with this method is permanent and destructive. That means, once you save the file, you won't be able to undo the changes the next time you open the file. The second method to apply adjustments or edits is by using the layers. The editing done with this method is non-destructive. To make adjustments with this method, go to Layer menu in the Menu bar and then go to New Adjustment Layer. This time, you will notice that there are a total of 15 adjustments available instead of 22. However, all the essential adjustments are present in these 15.

After adding an adjustment layer, it will be shown in the layer panel above your image. The dialogue box for the adjustment that you selected will also appear next to the layer panel. Though there are many adjustments in the adjustment submenu, only a few are the most widely used. These are:

- Brightness/Contrast

- Black and White

- Levels

- Hue/Saturation

Let's learn these adjustments one by one, starting with the Brightness.

Brightness/Contrast

With this adjustment, you can control the brightness and contrast of your image. Simply select 'Brightness/Contrast' from the New Adjustment Layer. After selecting this option, you will see a new dialogue box near the layer panel with two sliders to adjust these two features (adjustments) of your image. Taking the slider to the left will decrease the value of the two adjustments while taking the slider to the right will increase the value. Values can range from -150 to +150 for Brightness, -50 to +100 for Contrast.

Black and White

This adjustment is used to turn a color image to a black and white image. This adjustment is the most powerful and effective way to create monochromatic images in Photoshop. To apply this adjustment, go to the Layers menu, then to New Adjustment Layer and select Black and White. After adding this adjustment, a new dialogue box will appear near the layer panels for you to create stunning monochromatic images. Now you can apply a new filter from the drop-down menu and can change the value of various colors with the help of sliders present in the dialogue box.

Levels

Levels are the most important and extremely powerful tool for adjusting the exposure problems and can also be used to correct the colors in the image. To apply this adjustment, simply go to Layer

Menu, then go to New Adjustment Layer and select Levels. Below is the nomenclature of the dialogue box for this adjustment.

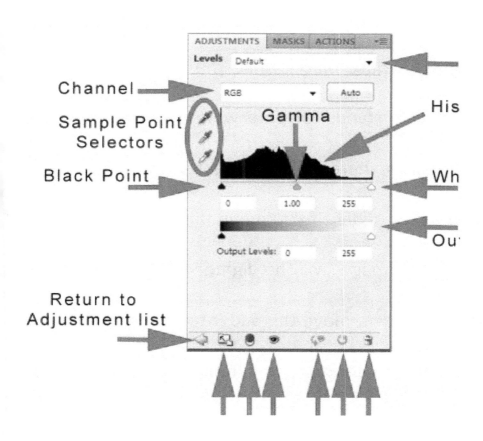

When you apply this adjustment, you will see a histogram. This histogram represents all the tonal values present in the image. The black point on the slider just below this histogram is set to 0 which stands for pure black, while the white arrow is on 255, which stands for pure white. Apart from these two arrows, there is the third arrow in the middle of the gamma slider. If you move this arrow to the left, then the image will be lighter in the mid tone, whereas if you move this slider to the right side, the image will be dark on the mid tone. Thus, the middle arrow on the gamma slider works differently from the other two sliders.

Sometimes, the black and white arrow does not coincide with the gamma histogram. This is shown in

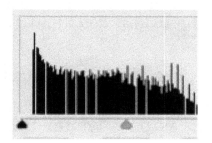

the image below.

This means that there are no true blacks or whites in the image, which may lead to a lack of contrast in the image. To correct this, we can move the arrows to meet with the histogram.

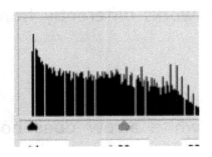

After correcting, the new values are 14 and 238. This means that the values less than 14 in the image will be shown as pure black and values greater than 238 will be shown as pure white. This is also known as mapping the values.

Hue/Saturation

This adjustment allows the user to manipulate the colors in the image both independently and globally.

To apply this adjustment, go to Layers Menu, then go to New Adjustment Layer and then select Hue/Saturation. After applying this adjustment, a new dialogue box will appear next to the layer panel with three main sliders. These sliders are Hue, Saturation, and Lightness. The Hue slider affects the color value of the image. Changing the color from the spectrum line will affect the coloring of the image. This adjustment is very useful when you use it for a specific color in the image. The Saturation slider represents the color intensity in the image. Moving the slider to the left will decrease the intensity of the colors and moving the slider to the right will increase

the intensity of the colors in the image. Moving the

slider to the extreme left will result in changing the

image into grayscale. The Lightness slider is clear

from the name and will change the lightness of the

image. However, using this slider is an advanced

technique and not recommended for beginners. This

is because using this slider improperly can result in

great loss of contrast in the image. Now, towards the

bottom of the dialogue box for this adjustment, you

will see an option called Colorize. If you will turn this

option ON, then the whole image in your Photoshop

screen will be tinted with a particular color. The Hue slider can still be used to change the tinted color and the Saturation slider can be used to change the intensity of the tinted color.

With this, we have completed the basic adjustments of the images that you can do with the help of Photoshop. Now, let's study a few more basic image editing options that are available in Photoshop.

Changing Size in Photoshop

When you are working in Photoshop, you can easily change the size of the image and the canvas that you are working on. To change the image size in

Photoshop, simply go to Image menu in the Menu bar, and select Image Size. After this, a new dialogue box will appear on your Photoshop screen where you can add the new values for the width and height of your image. Similarly, to change the canvas size, go to Image menu in the Menu bar, and select Canvas Size. After this, enter the new values for the canvas size.

The difference in Image size and canvas size is that, with image size, you will be able to change the size of the image that is there on your Photoshop screen, whereas, if you select the canvas size, it will add a blank area around the image (mostly white) if you increase the size, and will crop the image automatically if you decrease the canvas size.

Auto Tone, Auto Color & Auto Contrast

Photoshop has three automatic correction tools namely Auto Tone, Auto Contrast and Auto Color. With these tools, the user can improve the overall appearance of the image with a single click on the image. Let's discuss these three commands one by one, starting with the Auto Tone.

Auto Tone

This command automatically applies the Levels adjustment on the image with most accurate values which Photoshop generates based on its built-in intelligence. If you are looking to adjust the highlights, shadows or mid tones of an image, then Auto Tone is the best option for you to save you time.

Auto Color

This tool is mainly used to balance the color of the image. With Auto Color, you can adjust both the colors and contrast of the image based on the shadows and highlights. Using this command is helpful when you are trying to correct the saturation level in your image.

Auto Contrast

This command automates the Brightness/Contrast adjustment on your image. This tool makes changes to the image based on the overall color and contrast of the image rather than making adjustments to each color individually. This tool is useful in changing the highlights in the image to lighter and shadows to darker without changing the color values of the image.

Blurring the Image in Photoshop

In your Photoshop, you can easily create various types of blur effects on your image by activating the blur gallery filter and then using the on-image controls. In this section, I am going to tell you the basic method of blurring the images, which can be applied to all different kind of blur that are available in Photoshop.

To access the blur gallery, simply go to the Filter menu on your Main menu, and then go to Blur Gallery. You will see the following blue options there:

- Field Blur

- Iris Blur

- Tilt Shift Blur

- Path Blur

The method of blurring the image for all four types is the same and is discussed below:

- First open the image and create a duplicate of it by pressing Ctrl+J from your keyboard. This way, the original image will remain safe, and we can work on the duplicate copy for applying the blur.

- Next, go to the Filter Menu and then go to Blur Gallery. Now, select any of the blurs that you want to work with.

- As soon as you select a blur (Field blur for example), you will notice that an initial blur is applied to the whole image by Photoshop and the field blur options will appear on the right side of the screen. The initial blur applied to the image is applied uniformly all over the image by Photoshop and has a small circular icon over it. The circular icon is known as **Pin**. This icon is used to pin on the image. By default,

Photoshop adds one pin on the image but you can add multiple pins on your Photoshop.

- These pins actually control the amount of blur that is applied to the image at the area where the pin is placed. The pin controls the blur amount with the help of the outer ring present with the pin. If you move in a clockwise direction in the outer ring, it will increase the blur on the image. Similarly, if you move in an anti-clockwise direction, the amount of blur on the image will decrease.

- The blur slider provided in the blur options on the right side of the screen works just like the outer ring of the pin. You can increase or decrease the amount of blur by moving the slider to the right or left respectively.

- The initial pin and other pins that you add on your image for blur can be moved by clicking at the center of the pin and then dragging them.

- You can add more pins on your image by just taking your mouse cursor to the place where you want to place the pin and then making a simple click over there.

Blur may sound simple and easy but it is a very complex process to master properly. Let's now have a look at some of the shortcuts that you can use while creating images or designs in Photoshop.

Shortcuts in Photoshop

Using shortcuts not only saves a lot of time but also helps in maintaining your focus over long projects. Below are a few of the most widely used shortcuts in Photoshop:

Photoshop Result	Shor
Rectangular Marquee tool Elliptical Marquee tool	M
Lasso tool Polygonal Lasso tool Magnetic Lasso tool	L
Magic Wand tool Quick Selection tool	W
Crop tool Slice tool Slice Select tool	C K
Eyedropper tool	I
Spot Healing Brush tool	J

Conclusion

Photoshop is a vast software and discussing every single feature is beyond the scope of this book. I have provided you with a brief overview of Photoshop which will help you start using Photoshop today and also build your foundation for learning advanced Photoshop. But, this book is of no use if you are just going to read it and not practice the tools and adjustments that I discussed with you.

Open your Photoshop and start practicing today!

Happy learning!

Disclaimer

About The Author

John Slavio is a programmer who is passionate about the reach of the internet and the interaction of the internet with daily devices. He has automated several home devices to make them 'smart' and connect them to high speed internet. His passions involve computer security, iOT, hardware programming and blogging. Below is a list of his books:

John Slavio Special

Introduction

Photographs have been in fashion since they were known to the common man. People use photographs to capture and store their special moments. These photos help them in reliving those precious moments that they spent with their loved ones, friends, or family. But, it is not the 1940s or 1980s now. With time, people have developed various methods of processing images. Today, they capture images not only to remember their moments, but to share them with people on social media platforms like Instagram, Pinterest, Facbook, Twitter, and many others.

In my opinion, this is the very first reason today that almost all the gadgets are equipped with an in-built camera, and big brands like Apple, Samsung, etc., are competing with each other in terms of the camera quality for capturing images and videos. Thanks to these companies, today, almost everyone has a camera of their own, which was not possible a decade ago. However, having a camera does not make you a photographer.

Shooting random images or taking 'selfies' is very different from actual photography. You have to take care of various factors in photography which you don't even think about while taking a selfie. Photography is an art, a science and a process of creating amazing images using a digital device to record light.

The definition itself may sound confusing to some people who are new to photography. In this book, I am going to share various tips and tricks related to photography that you can use to capture various moments at different places with ease. All the tips that I will discuss in this book are based on my personal experience, and I believe that these will help you as much as they have helped me.

Capturing amazing images with the help of your camera is not enough. You need to produce some appealing images from those digital copies of yours as well. If you spend more than 30 seconds studying an image that you took, you will often notice that something is not presented the way you wanted it to be. You can always open such images in Photoshop to correct them and artificially improve them to make them better looking. Once you are done with the photography lessons in this book, you will continue learning about Photoshop and how you can use the same to make your images WOW!

Finally, I want to congratulate you for your purchase of this amazing book. If you follow this book properly, then you will certainly get a lot of value out of it as most of my other readers already have. So, let us start by learning about Photography.

The Basics of Photography for

Beginners

Okay, as I have told you earlier in the introduction chapter, the definition that I provided for photography can be confusing for some people. Keeping this in mind, I am going to tell you about photography from scratch.

Photography has really evolved with time and so have the terms related to it. Now, you do not need to remember all the terms and learn them by heart to become a good photographer. There are only a few basic terms that you will need to remember and understand to proceed with photography and this book. So, let us learn these terms –

Aperture

This might be the very first term that you will hear from a photographer, and this is why you should understand it at the beginning. In simple words, an aperture is known as the size of the opening of your camera lens. This is normally used to vary the amount of light in your image. If you think of the aperture as a window, then you can relate them easily. A big window will allow more sunlight to enter your room when compared to a smaller window in the same place. Aperture works in the same way by varying the size of your lens. An aperture which is opened widely will make your photos bright. Similarly, the smaller aperture will make your photos dark. Besides the amount of light, the aperture also influences the sharpness of your image. If the aperture of your camera is wide, then the background will be unfocused while a smaller aperture will give a comparatively sharper image.

Focus

This is another most common term among photographers. Focus is also another factor which affects the sharpness of your image. You can relate the focus of a camera with the focus of your eye. When your eye focuses on an object, then all the objects which are kept in that object tend to be blurry. You can check this by placing your palm in front of you and then focusing on it with your eyes. The focus of your camera works in the same way. All the objects which are in focus of your camera will be sharp, while the objects which fall outside the focus of your camera will be blurry. Today, all cameras are equipped with multi-focus, which allows you to focus on various images at the same time when capturing a photo.

Continuous Focus

You must be familiar with the autofocus function of your smartphone camera. It autofocuses on an object and continues to do so till you take the picture. However, there is a limitation to this function. If the object that you are currently focusing on, using the autofocus feature, starts to move; then the object will go out of focus. This is where the Continuous Focus option comes into play. With this option, your camera will continue to focus on the object, even if it is moving, until you click the image. Hence, helping you to get the sharp image that you desired.

Depth of Focus

Another important term related to focus. It is related to how much of the image is in focus, which is decided by the distance between the furthest and the closest object in the image. This distance is known as the depth of focus. For landscapes, the depth of focus distance is large. As a result of this, most of the images taken in landscape are in the focus of your camera. The portrait, on the other hand, has a shallow depth of focus, which makes the image looks soft rather than sharp.

Aspect Ratio

You must be familiar with this term as well; if not from your camera, then from the video player on your laptop or smartphone. Aspect ratio fits the video to the screen as per the ratio that you selected on your device. Aspect ratio is an important term related to photography and is often taken into account when printing the images that you captured. It is simply a ratio of height to width. Setting a proper aspect ratio for your image is really necessary to avoid the cropping of the image that occurs when you print it.

Burst Mode

This is one of the most amazing features and one of my favorite as well. If you want to take several images at once, then what you can do is keep clicking the images one by one with your camera until your collection is formed. Alternatively, you can use the burst mode of your camera. When you turn this mode ON, your camera will keep taking the images continuously while you are holding the image button down. How fast your camera takes these images depends on its speed. Some cameras are faster while others are slower. But still, it is the fastest method on your camera to take several pictures in a short time.

Bokeh

You must have seen this image or an image similar to this one on the internet. This kind of effect is produced with the help of light. Bokeh is the spherical shape created by light sources when they are kept out of focus in an image. This is achieved by widening the aperture of your camera. This is one of the most loved and neatest background effects used by photographers in their work.

Exposure

Exposure is a term related to image effects. Exposure means how light or dark your image is. An image is said to be a perfect one when the amount of light used is adequate. If the light is low in the image, then the image is termed as underexposed. When the light in the image is too much, then it is known as overexposed. I have already told you about aperture, which controls the amount of light in the image. Other important factors which decide the amount of exposure in an image are ISO and shutter speed. Let us now discuss these two terms.

ISO

ISO is the term which is given importance by professionals when they are deciding the exposure of light in their work. ISO decides how sensitive your camera is towards the light. You can change the ISO from the light sensor or simply the sensor option. This option is provided in the camera by default. A low value of ISO means that the camera is not very sensitive to the light. This kind of setting is used by professionals when they are taking an image in daylight. On the other hand, a higher value of ISO means that the camera is very sensitive to the light. This kind of setting is used by professionals when they are taking an image in an environment with low light. ISO needs to be configured properly when you are using your camera in low light; as using an ISO value which is too low can make your image look grainy. To prevent this, the ISO settings are always mixed with aperture and shutter speed to get the perfect exposure of the image.

Shutter Speed

Before discussing the shutter speed, let us first understand what a shutter is. A shutter is the part of your camera which opens and closes to let light get in, in order for you to take a picture. The speed in which the shutter opens and closes during this process is known as the shutter speed. The longer the shutter is opened, the more light will flow in, and vice versa.

Long Exposure

This is another term related to shutter speed and exposure. In this technique, the shutter of the camera is kept open for a longer duration; which helps you get a perfect low light image in an artistic way. This technique is often used by professionals during the night time to take amazing artistic images of the stars.

White Balance

This is **one of the most important terms** related to photography. When the light is low or high, your eye is able to adjust automatically to it. Your camera, on the other hand, cannot do this automatically. This is the reason why your images sometimes turn out to be a bit yellow or blue. To correct this and to take photos like a pro, you need to use the proper white balance in your images. Using the appropriate white balance value will make all the white objects appear white in the photos as well. You can use the automatic option for white balance which is present in cameras today. But, this option is not very accurate. Based on my own experience in photography, I advise you to adjust this setting manually.

Rule of Thirds

This is the most well-known rule of photography. I do not know a single professional who does not know this rule and does not use it in their work.

Why does every professional use this rule in their work? They use it because this rule works every time and helps them to capture professional images with minimum effort. If you are really serious about capturing images like a pro and you have very little knowledge about photography, then you should learn this rule by heart and implement it in your work. The basic idea behind the rule of thirds is to imagine the image that you see through your camera in 3 boxes, both vertically and horizontally, so that you have a total of 9 parts of your image. Now, place the point of interest of your image (that is the part of the image that you want to draw attention to) at the intersection point of the lines which are dividing your image horizontally and vertically into 9 parts. If you do this, then your image will be more balanced, and more the viewer will be able to interact more easily and vividly with your image.

So, that's it with the basics of the camera. If you understood the terms, then

I highly recommend you to go and practice these with your camera to polish

your photography skills. If you followed this chapter correctly, then you

should have already seen improvement in your skills. In the next chapter, I

will tell you about various other tricks that you can use to capture

professional looking images with ease.

Tips & Tricks for Capturing Images

Like Professionals

Okay, in this chapter, you will learn various tricks that I personally use to take amazing images. I am no professional but even so, most of my images are pretty decent. These tricks have helped me a lot, and they will help you as well; providing you follow this chapter thoroughly. So, without wasting any more time, let us begin with the tricks for awesome photography.

Never Underestimate the Manual Focus

Yes, I agree that we are living in the technology era and that people today trust the use of technology in their work more than anything else. But I still recommend that you use manual focusing instead of the automatic focusing when taking a photo with your camera. This is because; no matter how smart your camera is, its judgment of focus can never be fully accurate; especially in low light. Your camera will always struggle with focusing when you are taking a picture in the dark. Manual focusing, on the other hand, is an easy way out of this situation and plus; it is faster than automatic focusing. Let us take an example to understand more about manual focusing. Take a situation where you are taking an image of some birds sitting on the branches of a tree. In this case, your camera will mainly focus on the branches of the tree. Manual focusing, on the other hand, will allow you to have better control over your work in such situations.

The Half Shutter Method

If you like prefer using automatic focus, then make sure you do it right. Most newbies are unaware of the proper use of the shutter button. They think that the shutter button is only there for taking the image. **NO**, the shutter button works in two ways. If you press the shutter button to half, then your camera will lock all the settings, including the focus on the object. Once it locks it down, you will see a green signal or will hear a beep sound. This is to inform you that all the settings have been locked and you can now take the picture.

Then you should press the shutter button completely to capture an image. In case, you did not hear any such beep sound or did not see a green signal after pressing the shutter button to half; then it means that your settings were not locked by your camera and you should re-take it.

Throw Your Glasses Away While Photographing

Wearing glasses can sometimes turn out to be irritating and can also prevent you from capturing the perfect image. So, would it be worse to not use them while photographing? Yes, it is true. You can capture amazing images without wearing your eyeglasses. Every camera today has a small knob near the viewfinder of the camera. This knob is known as diopter adjustment knob. With the help of this knob, you can set the value of your eyeglasses in your camera and then can use it to capture the best shot.

Use Custom Settings to Save Time

If you use your camera to take images in the same environment and conditions, then you can set up the best settings and then save them in the custom settings of your camera. Every camera today has a custom setting option enabled. This will help you in taking professional images faster. For example, let us say that you take images of people in the same room every day with the same light amount. Then, instead of setting everything to the appropriate levels every time you take an image, you can set the settings once in your camera and can save them. You can then recall these settings with a click when you are ready to take another image.

Stick with sRGB Color Mode

sRGB is known as the standard color mode and is used in all digital works, including digital images, the internet, and printing. By default, your camera shoots in sRGB mode. However, there is another color mode which is known as Adobe RGB. This color mode has a larger color range than the standard sRGB mode, which influences the newbies to use it. However, no daily life gadget will show you the colors that will be recorded using the Adobe RGB mode. So, why would you even want to use them? I highly advise you to stick to sRGB when you are taking images.

Keep Your Camera Up to Date

Almost all the cameras that are available in the market today receive a frequent update from their respective companies to eliminate some errors which may be conflicting with the photo quality. Hence, it is always recommended to keep your camera's firmware up to date.

Use Fast Memory Cards

If you are a fan of the burst mode, then you should use a fast memory card in your camera. A fast memory card makes your camera's processing a lot faster than before; which improves the results of the burst mode. Most people today use a class 4 memory card. However, I personally use a class 10 memory card in my camera, and I recommend you to use the same. Many leading memory card developing companies, like San Disk, have developed even faster memory cards then class 10. Get those if you can. Just remember, the higher the class of your memory card is, the better the processing time.

Control the Camera Flash

Most of the cameras today have an inbuilt flash for photography. Although it is a good thing, using flash can damage the image quality by building harsh shadows, and that is why I recommend that you use a flash diffuser. The diffuser will soften the harsh flash light to help you take images professionally. If you do not have a flash diffuser with you, then you can simply cover the flash with a tissue paper (white in color). That will work pretty well.

Never Forget the Lens Hoods

Another common mistake among newbies today is that they ignore the use of a lens hood while taking a picture. I highly recommend you to use the lens hoods in your photography. It not only prevents your lens from the damage that can occur from the bumps, but it also eliminates the lens flare, hence improving the image quality to a certain level.

Always Use a Grip

There are times when you will have to use the longer lens in your work. In such cases, you should always use a camera grip to balance the weight of your camera. Moreover, whether you use a longer lens or not, using a grip is always known to improve the image quality in portrait mode, so why ignore them at all?

Use the Auto Distortion Correction Tool

As the name suggests, this tool helps in correcting the distortion automatically. Various lens kits which are available today have some kind of distortion because of the optical elements. This distortion can be easily eliminated using the auto distortion correction tool. Almost all cameras have this feature today. If you are about to buy a camera, then I recommend that you check the gadget for this feature.

Use Slow Sync for Better Exposure

If you take images in the darkness, then you may sometimes find yourself in a situation where the object that you are focusing on has appropriate light while the background remains the dark. In such cases, you can use the Slow Sync feature which is available in the flash menu of your camera. When you turn this feature ON, then your camera takes two exposures which are then blended together to present you the final image. It is recommended to keep your camera still while using this feature.

Take Care of the Sensor

Always keep your camera's sensor clean and free from any kind of dirt and dust. If you do not do so, then you will see some particles in your images because of the dust present on your sensor. You can also clean your sensor yourself. if you are unsure about it, then I recommend you to go to a professional to get it cleaned.

Never Underestimate the Histogram

Being able to know the exposure quality of your image is one of the best features of digital cameras today. However, some of the newbies and even professionals ignore the use of the histogram. As soon as you click an image, you can view it instantly with histograms to check the exposure. Most of the cameras today have a total of 4 histograms to tell the photographer if their image is underexposed, overexposed, or well exposed.

Now, it is time for you to pick up your camera and try these new tips and tricks yourself. Speaking of amazing images, one term that strikes my mind is perspective. We all know what perspective is, however, in photography we use forced perspective to generate amazing images. I will tell you more about forced perspective in the next chapter of this book.

Perspective Tricks to Shoot Images Like a Pro!

Okay, so let us start by understanding what forced perspective really is. It is a primary photography technique which is used by professionals all over the world to generate illusion in their work. This illusion is applied to make objects small or large in their photography. When used correctly, the concept of distance also becomes fun and easy with forced perspective. The forced perspective is used to create effects which are logically impossible in actual life. For example, showing one person in a gigantic shape in the image. Let us learn a few perspective tricks that will help you to shoot images like a pro! These tricks can also be used to create videos with amazing perspective effects. So, let us start!

Understand the Importance

Usually, people either give importance to what is in the background, or to what is in the front of it. In forced perspective, if you will have to give importance to the both of these equally. Giving equal importance to objects of different sizes is the first priority of creating illusions.

The Position of the Objects Matter

Where you keep your objects matters a lot when creating illusions. If you place your objects to the last column of the Rule of Third, then your image will be more balanced and more appealing in creating illusions. Take a look at the image below for example.

Using Zoom to Connect the Images

It is highly recommended to use Zoom to connect the objects in the images

together. If you work in high zoom, then you can easily connect different

objects in your image together as you will have more freedom to do so to get better results. Doing so will also give you more freedom in creating the size illusion when clicking the image from your normal eye level. Take the below image as an example.

Play with Point of View

Depending on how you use the point of view, the objects in your images can be changed to small or large length. For example, if you are closer to one object than the other, then the first object will appear larger compared to the second. Also, there will be a big variation in the length of the objects based on the height at which you capture the image. If the height of your point of view is less than the height of the object, then the object will appear large in your image. Similarly, if the point of view of your camera is placed at a height greater than your object, then the object will appear to be small in height. Below is an example for the same to help you understand better. In this example, the object seems greater than its actual height and also larger than the man.

Focus is the Evergreen Element

It does not matter if you are using the forced perspective tricks or are simply capturing an image, the focus always matters. However, it matters a little more than usual when we are using it to apply the forced perspective in our images. Most beginners take images applying the forced perspective which seem fake. Why? Because they simply ignore the concept of using focus in

146

forced perspective. Based on my own experience, I recommend you to use focus in all your perspective illusions. You will have to take care that the focus on both the objects of your image, with whom you are creating an illusion, is equal. If the lighting of the objects is not same, then your work will start looking fake. Always remember that a perfect illusion is the one which succeeds in fooling the human eye to believe what is in the image.

Here is an example of the use of perfect focus to correct the light exposure of the objects while creating a perfect illusion.

So, how well did you understand the concept of forced perspective and how to use it in your work to look like a pro? Do not know yet? Then it is time for you to go out and use it in your work. The more you practice, the better you understand, and better your work will be. In the next chapter of this book, I will tell you how you can use the various kind of filters to add artificial effects in your images.

Using Filters to Shoot Images Like a Pro!

I do not know a single professional who will not play with artificial effects to create amazing images. All photographers use some sort of filter in their work to create artificial special effects to make their work unique and more appealing to the viewers. In this chapter, you will learn the most popular filters used by professionals. So, let us begin!

Using the Cross Star Filter

This is by far the most used filter among photography enthusiasts. The cross star filter can be used to create a star-like illusion out of light sources. Depending upon the cross star filter you have, the filter will turn the light source into a 4 point or 6 point star. Notice here that I am talking about the light source and not the light. If you look at a cross star filter, then you can easily see a pattern which is responsible for capturing the light source and for turning the same into a star. This filter is mainly used to add a little charm to the image without making it look fake. For the best results, I recommend using this filter when there are 3 or less light sources. This is because more light sources can distract the viewers. Or else, you can use it when the light sources are at an appreciable distance from each other.

Using the Center Spot Filter

This is another popular filter used by professionals to play with focus.

Although everyone likes to click the sharp images, there is a special place in

photography for soft images as well. The images with soft parts are more

artistically appealing. The Center Spot Filter is used to create softness at the

edges of the image while keeping what's at the center of the image sharp.

This filter is often used when your object is in the middle column of the rule

of third. Using this filter allows the photographer to make a dreamlike

artificial effect. Below is an example to help you understand this filter more

clearly.

Using the Fog Filter

You can easily depict from the name itself that what this filter does. The fog filter adds fog as an artificial effect to your image. When you use the fog filter, the contrast of your camera is reduced which causes the incoming light to burst, hence creating a fog-like an effect in your images. This filter is often used to add a foggy morning effect in a landscape. You can also use this filter during the night. When doing so, the filter will make the stars appear bigger than their actual size and will help you in capturing their vivid colors. Filters are available in various intensities today: the 'A fog filter' has less fog intensity while the 'C fog filter' has high fog intensity. When using the fog filter, it is advised to adjust your aperture accordingly as the wide opening of the aperture can diminish the effect of the fog filters. Here is an example for you to see how this filter works.

Using the Multi-Vision Filter

Cloning an object was a pain before, but today, with the help of multi-vision filter, you can easily multiply the object without any problem in your image. These filters are often circular in shape and are made up of two pieces. You can multiply the object from 2 to 6 times by rotating the first element of the multi-vision filter. This filter comes with 2 simple modes, namely circular and linear. In linear mode, the object will be multiplied in a straight line, while in circular mode, the same will be multiplied in a circular form.

Using the Infrared Filter

The infrared filter has always been in fashion for photography. Mainly because the infrared lights are not visible to the naked human eye. The camera, however, can easily see these infrared lights. The infrared filter is used by photographers to block any light which lies outside the infrared spectrum. This enables them to capture an image in a dramatic and smooth manner. Infrared filters are also known for increasing the contrast of the image which is impossible to achieve in any other filter. When you use infrared filters in your work, you are advised to use a long exposure time; this is because, in the infrared filter, most of the light is blocked, which can make your image look darker. Below is an image which was shot with the use of the infrared filter.

I hope you enjoyed the example images that I provided in this chapter to explain the various kinds of filters. You can always use a filter to make your image more appealing. If you do not want to use a filter, then you can easily use something like a candy wrapper to add an effect. Below is an example where the photographer used the pink candy wrapper to cover the bottom part of the lens to create a pinkish bottom for the image.

The End of a New Beginning

So, that's it with the photography lessons. If you have followed the book thoroughly till now, then you can easily see the improvements in your work. From now onwards, it is all about how passionate you are towards photography, and how much time you want to devote to practicing your skills. The more you practice, then better you will become at it. Now, we will start with the second part of this book, which is about Photoshop and how you can use it to create amazing images. Let us first start with the general introduction of Photoshop.

Introduction to Photoshop

Photoshop was launched in February 1990 and its launch entirely modified the manner in which digital pictures were handled. It caused a revolution within the world's artistic community and created a very easy method for everybody to edit pictures without forcing them to buy expensive equipment from the local stores. The revolution started with Photoshop in 1990 continues to be alive nowadays as well. There are many other image editing software programs available in the market like Paint.net, but still, Photoshop provides the simplest flexibility and freedom in modifying images the way a user wants to. This is the main reason why, even after competition with several companies for over twenty-two years, Adobe Photoshop continues to be the worldwide standard for each company to edit and build pictures.

Over the years, Adobe has added additional options to Photoshop, to make it more awesome than before. In this section of this book, you will learn the basics of Photoshop and how you can use this amazing piece of software to edit the images the way you want.

Understanding the Photoshop Screen

Before you can begin using Photoshop to edit the images, you need to understand how the Photoshop screen looks. It is important to know what lies where on the screen so that you can easily access everything that you want without wasting any time in finding them at the last moment. The Photoshop screen that you see once you start the software is known as the Photoshop Workspace. Although you can easily customize this workspace to fit your editing style, for the sake of keeping this book simple and easy for beginners, I will be explaining the default workspace that you see after opening the Photoshop. You will see various tools that Photoshop provides to its users for editing and creating purposes at the left side of the screen. The right side of the screen is mainly occupied with Photoshop panels. These panels have extra options for the tools you use and have various sections to help you keep the track of your work (layers and artboards). At the top of the screen, you have the menu bar from where you can access additional features like Transform, wrap, etc., which are not available from the left or right panels which are provided by default.

Below is a screenshot of the Photoshop workspace to help you understand it better.

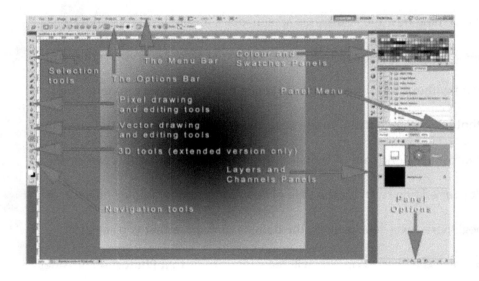

As you can see, both the left and right side tools and options are divided into various categories. For example, selection tools, navigation tools, layers, panels, color swatches, etc. Photoshop groups up the different tools according to their use to make it easy to remember where they are. This saves time in searching for tools in the Photoshop. In the next chapter of this book, you will learn about the toolbar, which provides various tools to the users for editing and creating purposes. Which will then be followed by the editing tutorials.

Understanding the Basic Photoshop

Tools

All the basic Photoshop tools are provided in the toolbar section. Also known as the tool panel, this section is located on the left side of the Photoshop workspace by default. You can click and drag it to a new place if you want to. The toolbar section contains many mouse-based tools that a user can select while working in Photoshop for editing and navigating purposes. In the above workspace image, I have already named the various sections of tools that are present in this toolbar (like selection tools, navigating tools, etc.). If you look at the toolbar section closely, you can easily see that these sections are separated by a small line. The first group of tools is selection tools, which are followed by pixel editing tools, vector editing tools and navigation tools. After these sections, you will see a color picker at the bottom of the toolbar and an icon that allows you to enter the quick mask mode. This mask mode allows

you to create selections for image editing. I have provided the burst view of

the toolbar to help you understand about different groups and their

respective tools.

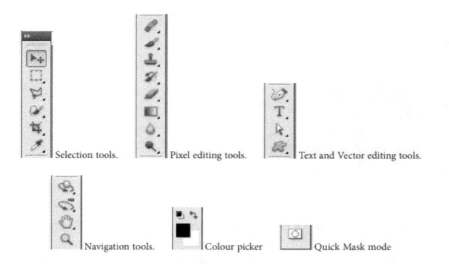

In the above image, you will notice that most of the tools have a small black

arrow at the bottom right. Most beginners ignore this arrow icon. This icon

actually means that there are more tools that can be accessed by the user by

clicking and holding the tool. Once you do that, a list of extra tools will

appear. Once the list appears on your screen, you can release the mouse and select the tool that you want to use; the list will remain until you make a

selection or click anywhere else on the screen. An example of the extra tools

list is shown in the image below.

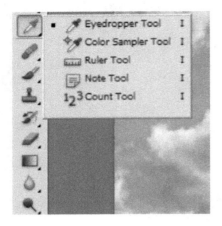

Now, let's learn about some of the most common tools used in Photoshop

for editing purposes. It is recommended that you open these tools and try

using them as you read about them for better understanding. This is the best

way to learn about any software that you want to.

The Move Tool

This is the most widely used tool in Photoshop or in any other image editing software available. You can move objects around the Photoshop workspace using the move tool. Click on the object to select it for moving, then click and drag to take it to its new position.

The Marquee Tool

The next most widely used tool for editing purposes is the marquee tool. The user can select the canvas in a shape of this choice. A rectangular shape is a default, but the user can change to an ellipsis shape if needed.

The Lasso Tool

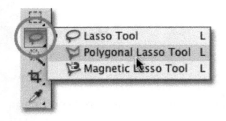

This is the tool which gets all beginners excited in Photoshop. Most users

start selecting with Lasso Tool even in the case where a marquee tool can be

used. The lasso tool lets you choose different parts of the canvas like a lasso,

in a free-form manner. You can also select the polygonal lasso or a magnetic

lasso tool from the extra tool list as shown in the image above. The magnetic

lasso automatically detects edges for you.

The Magic Wand Tool

This tool makes selecting and editing easy when an area of similar color is to be selected quickly. This tool can be used as an 'out of the box' method to remove backgrounds from photos. Using this tool makes Photoshop select the spot that's selected and anything around it. However, this tool should not be used when you have very little difference in the color. For example, this tool will treat the white and light gray in the same manner. If you go to select the white object, it will automatically select the light gray as well.

The Crop Tool

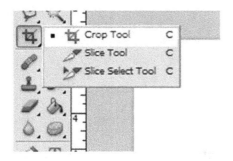

You must have used this tool on your smartphones. This tool is used to crop or cut a picture in Photoshop to any size that you wish.

The Eyedropper Tool

The Eyedropper lets you pick any color in your foreground or background as your selected color.

The Healing Brush Tool

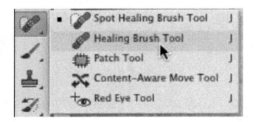

This is another famous tool for intermediate users of Photoshop. This lets you use part of the photograph to paint over another part. Photoshop will blend the surrounding areas of the picture as required.

Pencil and Paintbrush Tools

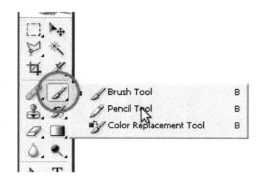

This is being used as a pencil. It can be adjusted to various sizes and shapes.

The Eraser Tool

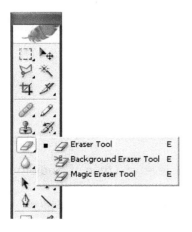

This is another tool that you must be familiar with because of the Paint

application on your desktop or laptop. The eraser tool is almost identical to the paintbrush tool in Photoshop. The only difference is that it erases instead

of painting a canvas.

The Paint Bucket & Gradient Tool

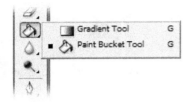

Again, the paint bucket is already known to you, but the gradient tool is a

new term for you, right? I am going to explain both of them simultaneously,

so you will understand better. The paint bucket tool works in a similar

manner to the paint application and lets you fill it in with a certain

foreground color. The gradient tool will blend the background with the

foreground by creating a gradient. You can choose level and type of gradients

required. These preset gradients are available in two or more colors which

you can use.

The Pen Tool

Suppose that the magic wand tool was of no help in changing the image's background because the background and image were very similar in color (like I said for the white and light gray color). In such cases, using a pen tool acts as a life saver for Photoshop users. Mastering the pen tool is the most challenging part for Photoshop beginners. But believe me, once you start using it, you will love it. As this tool is really important for Photoshop users, let's learn how to use it in detail.

To start with the Pen tool, open an image with a basic shape in Photoshop. Now, select the pen tool and click to create the edges of your shape. After completing it, you will see a little O if you hover over the first point. You can then click on that first point to close the shape. Hold ALT/OPT and click on a point to turn it from a curve to a straight line, and vice versa. It sounds really simple, doesn't it? But once you start using it, you will understand how much patience is required to master this small yet important tool.

The Text Tool

You must be familiar with this tool from the paint application on your desktop. However, the text tool is a little bit advanced in Photoshop. The text tool in Photoshop allows you to write in two different ways. It is really important that you understand both of these. The first way is how most people use text, by using what is called the Point text tool. You simply click on the Text Tool in the tools palette, click back on your image and start typing. The other way is to click on the Text Tool if it's not already clicked. Take the text tool and DRAG it out to make a rectangle. Now, you will be able to type in this rectangular box, and all the text that you type will be constrained by this box. This is known as Paragraph text. The paragraph text can be aligned in the box to the left, right, center or justify format as per your needs. One of the advantages of having a Photoshop CC version over Photoshop CS version is that CC support offers more fonts than CS version of Photoshop.

The Shape Tool

This tool makes creating simple shapes easy. With this tool, you can create rounded rectangles, vector rectangles, circles, polygons, custom shapes and lines. These shapes are very helpful when designing or creating shape masks for photos.

I hope that you have learned these tools by heart. Getting a good hold over these tools will help you in using Photoshop easily. Not only for editing the images but for creating new artworks as well. From the next chapter, we will begin our lessons on image editing as discussing every single basic aspect of

Photoshop is beyond the scope of this book.

The Concept of Color Grading

Color grading is a process where the colors of an image are enhanced and altered to create visually appealing and dramatic work. This technique is applicable to all digital media: like images and videos. In fact, all the movies that you see and images that you like always go through color grading before being presented to the world in their final version. Color grading helps in correcting the color of the image and to add artistic effects to it. Below is an example of a screenshot from the movie House On The Pine Street, to show you how color grading actually works.

The image above is presented without any color grading. Now, look at the image provided below to see how amazingly the color grading alters an image.

Did you see the difference? How amazing will it be if you can do this with the images yourself from your laptop? Well, that is possible, and it is exactly what I am going to teach you now.

The Color Grading Tutorial for Beginners

Okay, so before moving on, I want to tell you that to achieve good results in color grading you can use some settings in your camera to get the most stable images for this process. Below are some of the settings that I personally use in my camera while taking photos.

The Camera Settings for Color Grading

Always use a large aperture on your camera while taking photos. A value between f/1.4 and f/2.0 will do it. What we are trying to do here is to generate a bokeh effect, that is, blur what is in the background while having the things in the front stay sharp. I have already covered bokeh in the previous chapters of this book.

Light always plays an important role in the images. Having a shadow is often recommended rather than having a pale image of someone's face with no shadows. The shadows, however, need to be soft and not harsh. To achieve this, you can either use the artificial light, a flash diffuser (I have explained it already) or you can simply click the image immediately after sunset to get soft shadows.

These tips will always help you to capture the image in the most cinematic way possible, without any external help.

Now, let us learn how you can use color grading in Photoshop to enhance your images.

Color Grading in Photoshop

Color grading is done in Photoshop with the help of layers. Over the image, we keep adding several adjustment layers to apply the various effects. To those who are unfamiliar with layers, they are simply a collection of objects, or text, in Photoshop. When you place these layers one over the other, you get a full image. Here is an example –

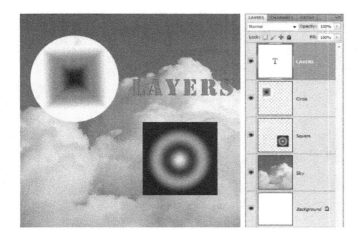

In the image above you can see that the full image is made up of 5 layers.

Each layer can be individually edited to edit the image. The final result of the

same is shown in the main Photoshop workspace. Now, let us move towards

color grading. I am going to use the following image to teach you about the

color grading process.

We will add color effects to this image by enhancing the yellow color in the highlights and green color in the shadows. So, let us begin!

Firstly, open the image in the photoshop, it will be shown with the name – background, with a lock sign over it. Now, you need to right-click on this layer and select the option which says 'duplicate the layer'. This will make a copy of the image which you can edit. This is done so that you can preserve the original image in case you don't like the editing that you did on its copy. You can then use the original image to make a new copy to begin editing.

We will now add an adjustment layer to this image. To do so, go to the menu bar and click on layers, then select the new adjustment layer. A new side list of commands will open in front of you, from here, select the Color LookUp

option as shown in the image below.

A new dialogue box will appear in front of you to enter the layer name, you can enter whatever you like. To keep track, I usually use the Color Look Up to remember what this layer is doing. Below the name field, you will see the opacity option. I recommend using 20% as the opacity value for the work. Otherwise, the effects that you will add will be too strong. After adjusting the opacity, all you need to do is to hit enter to add this layer. Now, open the layer properties for editing. To do so, you can right click on the color look up layer and select edit adjustment. Now, for the 3DLUT file option, select filmstock_50.3dl.

Now, the next step is to enhance the image with the help of curves adjustments. To do this, add a new curve adjustment layer. Go to layers -> New Adjustment Layer and then select curves. For the use of curves, you can keep the opacity to 100% so that they can redo the contrast of the image properly. After adding the curves layer, open the properties and you will see a graph with a curve from bottom left to the top right corner. How much contrast you want in your image depends on you, and you are free to adjust it according to your needs.

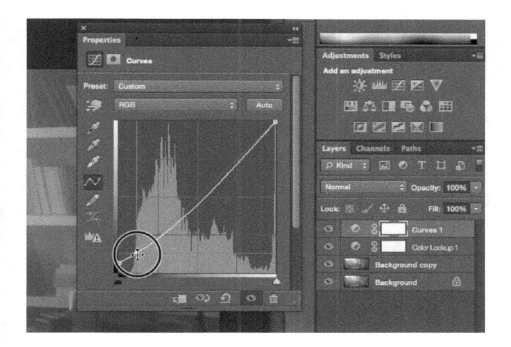

After adjusting the contrast, we will add another curves adjustment layer with 100% opacity. In the properties of this new layer, instead of RGB, select blue. Now, lower the curve end from the top right corner as shown in the image below.

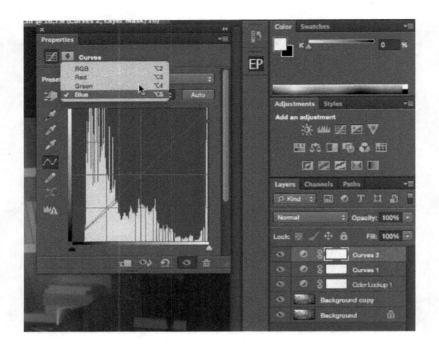

Doing so will add a yellow effect to the shadows present in your image. Once you are done with the adjustment according to your needs, you can proceed to add another adjustment layer with 100% opacity to adjust the overall color balance. To do so, you will need a color balance layer. Go to layers -> New Adjustment Layer and select the color balance. Open its properties to balance the yellow and green to add effects to your image. Here is what your screen will look like once you open the properties –

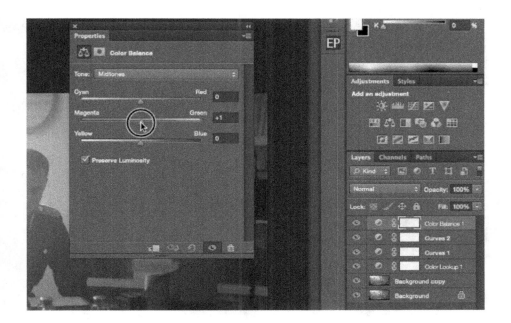

In the tone tab, select Midtones and change the amount of green color in your image. This will enhance the shadows of your image. Now, from the tone option, select the Highlights and adjust the yellow color to enhance the light in your image as shown in the image below.

Now, let us lighten up the image a little. To do so, add another curves layer with 100% opacity and adjust the graph for RGB to increase the amount of light in your image. In case you want to darken your image, you can follow the same, but instead of taking the curve towards up to add light, you will have to take it towards the bottom to darken the image. You can add these two images with the separate opacity to make an advanced effect on your image.

After doing all the steps, here is what my image looks like. In the next

chapter, we will learn what photo manipulation is and how we can combine

the two images to create a single cool-looking picture.

Photo Manipulation

Photo manipulation is nothing but another effective technique which is used by professionals for creating amazing images. It is a process which involves various operations (example color grading) to add the desired changes to the photographs. Photo manipulation is widely used today for works included in advertisements, promotions, magazines, artworks, etc. In professional language, it is known as retouching the images to enhance their visual appearance. One of the most used photo manipulation techniques is to combine the two images to make an amazing picture. Let us see how it is done.

Let us combine the following two images to create a cool looking picture.

Now, start by opening the first file in Photoshop. To edit the image, right click on the layer named background in the Photoshop layers panel and then select 'convert to smart object' as shown in the image below.

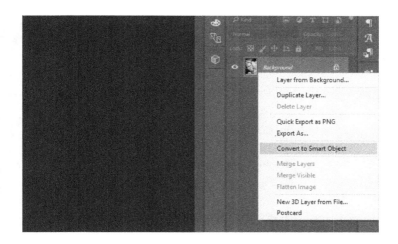

Now, add the second image file to the first file. You can simply drag the second image from the file explorer and release it in Photoshop over the first image. It will look something like the screenshot below –

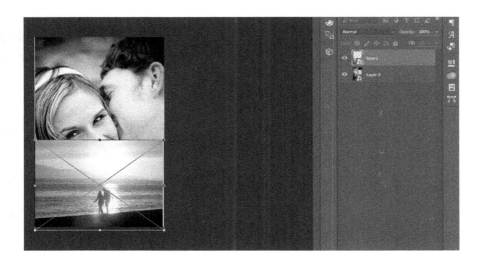

Now, hit enter to place the image there. Once you place the image, you can use the move tool to get the image to the bottom, as shown in the screenshot above. Now, hit the Ctrl+T from your keyboard to launch the free transform tool. Now, resize the bottom image so that its width is as much as the width of the first image, as shown in the screenshot below.

Now, we will use the same free transform technique on the first image to change its position. To make sure that you do not alter the image height to width ratio accidently, and that you move it in a straight line, I recommend that you hold the shift key while operating.

So, hold the shift key and move the image a little higher to get the results shown in the screenshot below.

Here you can see that the face of the woman is fully visible now, whereas the man's hair is not. The point here is to get what matters from the image inside the working frame so that it is completely visible. For me, the face of the woman was more important than the man's hair.

The next thing that you need to do is to create a layer mask over the second

image (that I, the one with the sunset). To do so, select the marquee tool

with the second image layer set as active, then select the whole image. Now,

go to layers -> Layer mask and click reveal all. You will now see an additional

layer has been linked to the layer of the second image, as shown in the

screenshot below –

Note here that the layer mask is shown with the white background with a

border around it. If you do not see anything like that and see just a white background without border, it means that you have linked a layer and not a layer mask. You should only and only link the layer mask.

Now, let us start blending the two images with the help of this layer mask. From the toolbar, select the gradient tool and then from the options bar, which is just below the menu bar at the top of your screen, select the black to white gradient. Below is an image to help you out on this –

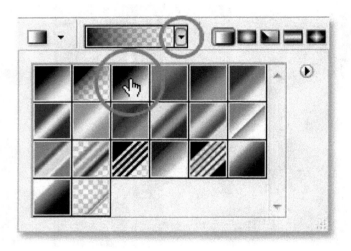

Now, click anywhere else on the screen (not on the image) to close the options. Now, go back to the image, select the layer of the second image linked with a layer mask. And then, holding the shift button on your keyboard, click and drag along a line on the second image, as shown in the image below –

Once you reach the bottom end of the line, release the mouse to apply the gradient effect to your image. It will look similar to the screenshot shown below –

Now, we are done with the combining and editing part of the image. Now we can merge these two layers together to create a single image out of them. To do so, select the two layers from the layers panel and then right click and select – Merge Layers. Photoshop will now create a new layer for this purpose. Now, we can continue to add the color of our choice to this image.

To do so, we will first have to desaturate the image to change it to black and white. To remove all the color from your image hit Ctrl+Shift+U from your keyboard. You will now see a desaturated image like the screenshot below.

Now, you can add a new color layer to add a color of your choice. To do so, go to layers -> New Fill Layer and then select the Solid Color option. As soon as you do this, you will be provided with the color dialogue to select the solid color for your image. I selected the purple color, and the results of this action are shown below –

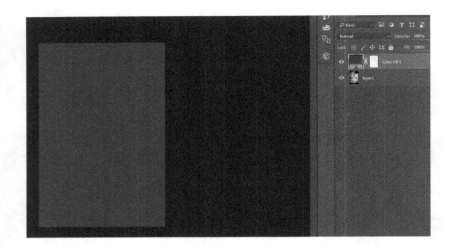

You can see that my whole image was covered with the purple color. Now comes the interesting part. Now, we will change the blend mode of the color layer from Normal to something else. In the screenshot below, I changed the blend mode to screen from normal –

For the same layer, I changed the blend mode from screen to subtract to get

a cool greenish effect on my image. Here is a screenshot to help you

understand –

With this, we have reached the end of the chapter on photo manipulation and how to combine the two images to create a single cool image. I hope that this chapter was useful for you.

Conclusion

So, we have come to the end of my book on Photography and Photoshop. I hope that you enjoyed it and learned a lot from it at the same time. Like anything else, both Photography and Photoshop require time. The more time you give to them, the faster you will improve your skills. Finally, I again want to thank you for purchasing this book. I have done my part, and now it's your turn. So, get started with Photography and create some amazing images out of the pictures that you capture.

Good Luck!

Techniques Using Photoshop

Introduction to Photoshop

A History of Photoshop

Photoshop goes back a long way in computer history, starting out in 1987 when it was *sold* to Adobe. That's right, even though this wonderful software was not an idea generated by Adobe, they saw the importance of Photoshop right from the beginning. It was originally called displayed and the original creator, Thomas Knoll, needed some encouragement from his brother for the program to become a fully-fledged photo editing software. Even though Photoshop was developed in 1987, the first official release didn't come out until 1990 where it sold for $300 an hour. Accounting for inflation, that would be $559.15 an hour in today's money, which would pay for nearly 4 years of the newest Photoshop from the web.

Originally, Adobe's concept of allowing for Cloud interfacing and the initial signs of no longer own any of the software began with the Creative Cloud. This concept was released in 2013 and not very well received by the community as it often caused complications with offline users and users who preferred to have the standalone version of the software as they had enjoyed for nearly two decades beforehand. This led to many reverse engineering the CC software to block the subscription service and the branding came under some severely negative press. The problem with Adobe at that point though was that so much of the industry relied on these tools that they really had nowhere to switch to when the company started doing things that the consumers didn't like. As a result, many of the original users just renewed out of a forced decision to either use the software or make due with the many bug-ridden copycats of its time. Back then, software like Gimp and Sony Vegas were extremely limited in what they could do. The criticism was so significant that it managed to receive a petition to change it and the petition received 30,000 signatures to do so. On top of this, the Creative Cloud was not perfect in anyway as many found that the file syncing was broken and that there was a common worry that independent users like ourselves would be forced to upgrade when certain features rolled out.

The truth of the matter is that I find the next part rather hilarious because the company thought that making it an online service would bring down piracy, but then they got hacked and all the services were released the very next day. I find this ironic, as I have always seen piracy as more of a marketing tool to get the word out about software since pirates will usually talk about good software to their friends. On top of this, most pirates that steal the software usually just steal software because they want to try it out first to see its worth the money they're asking for it. What companies never tell the public is that piracy goes significantly down when there is a trial version of the software out for use by the general public. One day they may learn that piracy is a potential tool, but, until then, it is up to the companies to decide how much money they want to lose in their fight against piracy, which will always be something that's possible in the digital world.

What Version I Will Be Using and Why That Isn't An Issue

For all the lessons herein, I will be using CS5. I have been using CS5 near the beginning of its release and have used it to create book covers, edit family and professional portraits to severe extents at family request, and edit photos needed for the inside of books and articles. The camera that I use is a Nikon D3200, which is still a decent camera but it is falling off the quality scale so I will likely get a Canon Rebel Ti6, but personal camera selection aside, even though CS6 and "CSWeb" has been out for quite some time I still have not updated this software. This brings me to why the version of what Photoshop I am using will not matter for this book.

The symbols that represent the tools I will be teaching you how to use rarely change between the versions and their purpose rarely changes. In reality, the developers at Adobe cannot have their consumers constantly relearning software or other options like Gimp will be sought out as a much easier alternative. Each version has implemented changes but rarely is a tool taken out of the software in the same process and even rarer still is a basic tool removed, which will be the types of tools we review here. Therefore, the version doesn't really matter so long as the version is between CS5 and up as CS4 and below may be lacking some of the tools added into CS5.

Additionally, even if you decide to use a free open source software like Gimp later on down the road you can bring what you learn from this software over to that software. The symbols used to represent the tools may change between software but you will find that many of the tools are the same. This is because the tools are based in art and art techniques, which rarely change over time but do occasionally improve. This allows many artists to pick up different software and become acquainted with that software rather quickly.

Therefore, as I have stated before, the tools I may be using for this may change symbols but you can bring this knowledge to nearly any new *good* image manipulation software. As for what Gimp is, if you don't already know, it is the Linux equivalent of Photoshop since Adobe did not create a Linux friendly version of their software for the longest time. Adobe developed "CSWeb" or the online creative suite because it wanted to make sure that its software was healthily protected against piracy. However, Adobe unknowingly gave into pirate demands because many pirates only stole the software because they didn't see how a company could justify charging consumers thousands of dollars for software that has only ever increased in quality by a small increment. By charging a relatively cheap subscription fee, the new Adobe suite now aligns itself in a more affordable layout than previous versions.

The Basic Layout Left to Right

Let's go over the basic layout before we go over some important facts about Photoshop and then dive into the basic toolset itself. Below you will find a screenshot of my tools in as small a window as possible so that it can fit inside of this book.

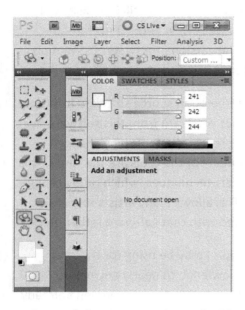

In the top left corner, we have the Photoshop logo to remind us who to thank for creating so many wonderful pictures and for causing some of the most frustration we've experienced in our lives. On this line, we have a bunch of extra environments we could be working in but we do not need to worry about that. Below this, we have the File "and more" bar, which is an area that is more suited toward the advanced Photoshop developer since there are options like Liquify and Vanishing point, which are some nifty but definitely tricky first time features of the software to use. Below this bar, you have the "Current Action" Bar, which is not a literal name but a figurative name. The first box you see on the left side of the canvas that has a square and a mouse with a directional symbol is called a tool bar. When you finally choose a tool inside of this toolbar, the "Current Action" Bar will update to show you a basic amount of things you can do with that feature of the program. Therefore, the "Current Action" Bar will show you what current actions you can take with this tool. This is very important to understand, as these two bars are bars you will be messing with **all of the time** while you are inside of Photoshop. To the right of all this are your primary organizational and manipulator tools. First, we'll start with color, which modifies the current color palette of the program. Therefore, if you switch over to brush and set those values inside the color box to green then the paintbrush will be green.

The category of swatches can be found next to it and swatches literally are the same thing as Color, but provide a set of preset colors instead of you just trying to create your own colors. As you can tell, the colors don't seem to be in order but these colors are organized to record the most common colors that a person will use.

Styles refers to the stylish brushes you can use while in Photoshop, but this is a much more advanced topic to cover as there are many different styles and styles are something that you can create on your own. In fact, there are many style sets out there for Photoshop just like there are brush sets, but these are all custom modifications that require a thorough knowledge in order to put them into use. Below this box is a box that contains Adjustments and Masks. We will cover Adjustments later in this book, but these are the primary tools you use to manipulate photographic elements.

Masks are an area of this program that we will work past because the topic of Masks can make their own book. Additionally, the box below that with the options of Layers, Channels, and etc. will be a box that we mostly avoid since you need to be making some significant changes to a photograph in order for that to come into use.

Layers will be where you hold sections of manipulated photographs whereas Channels are where you choose the different color channels to manipulate. This area, in general, is dedicated to selecting different "layers" of a photograph or multiple photographs, which is why I pointed out that you will likely not need to know more about this section until much later on in your learning experience.

Basic Photoshop Rules

Photoshop Cannot Edit RAW Images - Lightroom

Photoshop is not meant to handle RAW images for a very good reason. RAW images are raw and "unfinished" with a lot of data that's compacted into a small space. Photoshop is meant to manipulate and create finished pieces of Photography, which means the tools are built to handle images that are not in their raw form but, rather, in a state where each area is already digitally finessed. To many who have to deal with the two software, this sounds like a garbled mess that could be tidied up and to that I have to say: blame your camera's company. Lightroom was built to take advantage of each RAW format's most beneficial qualities, something that would be difficult to build into a long standing software like Photoshop. This allows Adobe to focus in on the purpose rather than removing features just to make the program manageable. The only reason why Adobe *had* to do this was because each company decided they wanted to enter the RAW format bidding war in the beginning and there was no industry standard set at the time. Therefore, Adobe didn't have the ability to fully implement all the changes each company made to their respective formats. To deal with that, Lightroom was created and now, as artists,

Photoshop Does Not Do Gif or Animated Photos - Fireworks

Photoshop is meant for *still digital* imagery and not much else. Sure, it can provide you with a few options to render as a 3D object and similar items, but these are all meant to work with you in the aspect of developing *still photographs*. This means that file formats that require multiple images in order to make the one image that simply won't work in Photoshop as this is handled by Fireworks. Fireworks is a Photo Animation software. This is very important to understand because Adobe gears their software develops around specific aspects of the industry. If Adobe were to combine all the elements of Photoshop with all the elements of Fireworks, we would have this massive program that took up a ton of memory and required you to spend at least a year in the basics just to get to the point where you were comfortable enough to move around in this type of space. This is where Adobe chooses to separate their software: this allows them to focus on features that are specific to that software's purpose.

Photoshop Takes A Lot of RAM

I'm going to show you the difference between two photos of different size and then of different format to show you how quickly Photoshop can become a RAM hogger. I'll also explain why RAM is important to you.

This first one shows a small file in the format of JPEG, which takes up very little RAM as we see here.

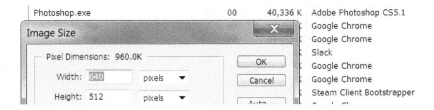

This second photo shows a very large file in the format of JPEG, which takes up nearly three times as much RAM.

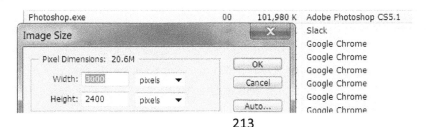

213

This third photo shows a very small file in the format of PNG, which only causes the RAM usage to rise by a small percentage.

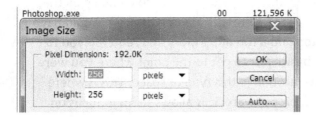

This last photo shows a very large file in the format of PNG, which causes a huge and noticeable impact on RAM usage.

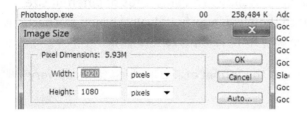

This additional photo is with one 3D modification added to that last photo to show the significant increase that manipulation causes.

Photoshop.exe   02   357,700 K   Adobe Photos

As you can see, the more complex we made the photo in terms of size and file format the more RAM was needed in order to render that to our screen. Once we made just a single modification, it became very evident that manipulating photos takes a lot more additional RAM usage than just loading the picture into Photoshop. Luckily, I work with about 12GB of RAM, so I don't have to worry very much about this but if you have one of those computers that only has 4GB of RAM, you may want to upgrade this to a higher amount as you will find that 4GB is simply too little to do a lot of manipulation with. On the other hand, if you don't get extensively into editing a photo then you will find that 4GB of RAM is the perfect size for you. However, let us talk about why I keep mentioning RAM in this section.

Why is RAM important?

RAM stands for Random Access Memory, which means it allows for the computer to Randomly Access Memory from the hard drive. This is what allows us to load files that we click on instead of loading everything in order to get to the file that we want to view. That file is stored inside of RAM and all of the modifications are also recorded inside of that RAM because you may want to change it, alter it further, or reverse what you have changed. This all leads to an increased build up in RAM usage and is the reason why you want to keep an eye on what it is using up that RAM. To make it even worse, when you try to do 3D manipulation, Photoshop is not designed to utilize the graphics card fully and relies on the PC to help with this, which is why you say that I went from using >1 cores to 2 cores. Once again, I run an octo-core computer so I am not worried but this would easily tap out a computer that is only a duo-core and even push the limits to a quad-core. This is why RAM is so important to those who intend to do any type of modifications inside of Photoshop.

YouTube Has All The Answers

I do not know how long YouTube will last, especially during the controversy that this book releases in, but YouTube is not the only video service on the market. With that said, YouTube has all the answers when it comes to manipulating specific aspects of a photograph or graphic. However, even though they may have all the answers, those answers still may not be adequate or what you want simply cannot be done in the program. An example where I encounter this all the time would be Adobe Premiere Pro, which is a powerful video editor but not the friendliest of software. When you speed up footage in Adobe Premiere Pro the audio pitch becomes a lot higher. However, if you were to try to fix this you would find that it is extremely difficult unless you recorded with this in mind. The ironic part is that there are plenty of YouTube tutorials on how to do this yet none of them ever seem to work for me. The same is true of the Magic Selection tool in Photoshop, which has never worked for me on the first go when I try to remove the background of a photo to switch it out. This is because the photography that they use in the video tends to be crystal clear studio footage or stock footage that has been thoroughly tested to be manipulated. Stock footage that cannot be manipulated is somewhat useless to most. The photography that I take can have blemishes in it and areas where I do not have enough data to manipulate the environment of my subject. This could be the certain lighting I thought would be nice causes a lack of data or an unforeseen wind blew some elements of the photo out of perspective and I couldn't see it until it wound up on the big editing screen that I use. Therefore, while YouTube may have the answers, you still need to take those answers with a grain of salt to get anywhere in most photography manipulation areas.

Quality Photos Make For Easier Manipulation

Trust me when I say that having poor photography to work with also means having very little to manipulate. You can try to fix the quality all you want, but unless the photo was clear from the get go there will likely not be a chance to ensure the photo looks like it was crystal clear. As you will come to understand, the pictures you take or someone else takes for you are literal snapshots of data. When you have a snapshot of poor quality this also means that your bucket of data will be considerably less than a bucket of high quality data. This means you could be at the point where you can't remove the background, remove a smudge in the face, refract the light differently by manipulating contrast, and many other manipulation methods to improve the look and feel of a photo. There simply isn't enough data to support your

216

actions and the only way to get such data is to retake the photo, which will likely be impossible if you have gotten to the point of editing the photo. This is one of the most frustrating things to accept as a photographer and the easiest way to prevent this is to make sure that you take more than one of the same picture. I personally love the new rapid-fire shutter speeds that come out on newer cameras as they tend to capture a lot with very little effort. Additionally, always make sure your target has the proper lighting because some of the data is lost when the target is just too dark or is just too bright for you to manipulate. Even though in color theory we learn that white is full of color and black represents the lack of color.

Understanding Formats

Why are formats important to photo manipulation?

I find this an ironic question that is asked by many new comers to the scene of photo manipulation. The truth of the matter is that file format represents the canvas type that you are using in the digital world. Just like some artists will use a rough canvas to give a more rustic or original feel to their medium, we, as digital artists, will use format for certain situations. Below, I will go over different e-file formats, what they do, what they are good for, and the cost of using that specific type of format.

Bitmap

Bitmap is the old king of kings as it were since Bitmap was once the only thing available to us. Bitmap refers to a mapping of bits. Bits are what we refer to when we are calling on a collection of computer data. The computer data we are talking about is a collection of three numbers, which make up the RGB system. That stands for Red Green Blue and it is important that you memorize this for later on down the road.

RGB is made up of three numbers. Each of these numbers go from one to two hundred and fifty five. Something like 0,0,0 is black while 255,255,255 is full of color, which would result in the color of white. These color combinations make up a bit of color.

The next part of Bitmap is the mapping part which comes in the form of the x and y axis. You see, even though you know the color you still need to know where that color is. The x and y coordinates come from graphing and since the computer is just a calculator and the screen is just a place for it to draw the result of our equations we must order our RGB into x and y coordinates so that the computer can draw it on the screen correctly. Luckily for us, someone already thought this up and called it Bitmap.

Bitmap is useful for Pixel Art, such as the one you see in many portable games of the retro era for gaming (the newer graphics allow for more visually entertaining). The bad part about Bitmap is that it doesn't provide a lot of color depth and enhancements that came in the format libraries released after it. It is, honestly, a format that is used less and less by consumers, but it is still in circulation due to mobile texts and other technologies that need to severely lower the size of, normally, large files.

PNG

PNG is perhaps the second most recent of these common file formats but tends to be one of the heavier file formats available to us. However, PNG offers a very important factor in photo manipulation and that would be *transparency*. Transparency allows web developers or web design to make Logos that do not have a background. Additionally, this feature allows us the ability to mix photos together and take a greater sense of control over our pictures. This does come at a cost though since the file sizes tend to be larger than both JPEG and Bitmap. This is not ideal for those who are worried about people visiting a website, so developers try to keep PNG's down to a minimum if at all possible.

JPEG

JPEG is the one I work with the most because it allows for a rather small file size without giving up too much quality. Likewise, there's a lot to be had when you see the difference between 4K RAW imagery and JPEG. JPEG was made so that we would have more advanced image processing than in Bitmap, but also maintain a low file size. This is why many of the images you see on the web are primarily made up of JPEG files. The JPEG file lowers the data needed to send it from the server to whatever device you are connecting. The two formats are heavily debated amongst developers and designers, but, unless you are making professional art, you will likely be using JPEG simply to save room on your computer since the difference between PNG and JPEG are very low, with transparency being at the forefront of the differences. With JPEG, you cannot use transparency in your photos and this is why some prefer to use PNG in their websites.

RAW

The last file format isn't really a format but, rather, a description of several types of formats. Nokia had its own format, Canon did too, and all the other companies that wanted to provide the best clear picture possible. In order to cope with all the different formats of RAW, we just all called it RAW and eventually some of the companies fell in line but RAW is much different than all the other formats. First, it is massive. Something that would normally be 12MB in JPEG or 24MB in PNG would be 120+MB in RAW. Those measurements are not exact and nor would the conversion be every single time. Secondly, it is incompatible with nearly every program that used to handle picture formats so new software had to be made. We'll talk about Adobe's version of a solution in a little bit, but Nokia (my D3200) decided to allow to convert it into JPEG and this was often the resounding response to RAW photos. However, RAW photos are specifically for real photos and the algorithm is designed to use capture the maximum amount of data it is supposed to capture.

Initial Setup

Finding Your Free Photos

There are many options when it comes to photography and I am not going to act like I'm a master when it comes to determining which photos follow what rules. What I am talking about is when you need a photo to begin editing and messing around with. Unless you have taken a recent photo with your phone, you will often find that you are editing online photos. In order to find the correct photos to edit, you need to know the internet media copyright laws associated with photographs.

Creative Commons

The creative commons copyright laws protect the common people's creative works. Normally there are additional stipulations for each one such as naming them when you use their photos, not using their photos for any commercial gain, or not modifying the photos when you get them. However, we're going to talk about the one you want.

Copyright Rules

CC0 is where the photo or artwork is in the public domain. As photo manipulators, we love CC0 medias as it means we do not have to credit anyone, it is completely free, and we can change the photo to our hearts content, which is why we are really here.

Now, the website I tend to use when I am looking for free CC0 photos is Pixabay, which is a common resource amongst web developer. The pictures found here are of a very high quality and tend to be similar to what you might find in a stock photo gallery. You can usually choose a specific size, so you can choose the best one for your computer.

Importing Your First Photo

Once you have selected a photo to manipulate, it is time to bring that photo into the Photoshop program for editing. In order to do this, you need to click on file and then on open.

Once you are in the file screen, you must navigate towards the file. Keep in mind that there are a lot of formats that Photoshop can handle so be sure to save your file in a location that you can easily find.

File name: wine-glasses-176991_640.jpg

Files of type: All Formats

Open

Cancel

Image Sequence

File Size: 123.1K

Likewise, if you hold shift or control while clicking on photos you will find that Photoshop allows you to open multiple photographs. Keep in mind that this will open them all in separate canvases. In order to mix photos together, you must first have the main image open and you must drag the additional image over that canvas. You will then be able to manipulate its size and set it into a more permanent place.

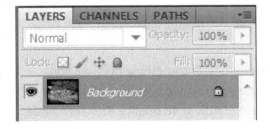

LAYERS CHANNELS PATHS

Normal Opacity: 100%

Lock: Fill: 100%

Background

One thing you will notice when you first open up a file image is that the file image often has a lock next to it. Double click on this in order to unlock it and then click "Okay" when the text dialog opens up. Photoshop first locks the photo to prevent any adjustments that may be errors.

Once you have unlocked the image, you can make all the edits you want to it but there's still a bit more than you will want to know about in terms of photos.

Photoshop File Sizes

Photoshop has certain sizes for the photos that it utilizes and saves, but this is really only a concern if you want to do some super sampling. Here are the sizes just to clear this up:

- .PSD - 30,000 x 30,000 and 2GB

- .PSB - 300,000 x 300,000 and 4 Exabyte

PSD is the extension your file will be save in most of the time and it will feel very common after a long while. With that said, PSD does have a limit, which is why PSB was developed. Now, PSB does have a limit but you are likely not going to reach it yourself unless you are an astronomer that's working on the innovative technology of tomorrow. However, PSD is something people have run out of before and this is due to two different types of technology along with one technique.

Super sampling is the art of taking the quality of something massive and rendering that quality on a smaller scale. For instance, you could have 4K pictures but you want to render them in 1080p at 4K quality. This technique was developed because rendering technology was up to date before television screens and computer monitors could render it. Therefore, the more fanatic of game players and media lovers chose to super sample in order to get the quality.

Now that 4K televisions have come on to the screen these same gamers and media enthusiasts are rendering 12K super samples. At the same time, the advent of the 360 imagery has come to life and now there are five pictures of 12K. Finally, we have conquered the PSD with a total of 60k being super sample for a 360 view. Therefore, unless you are planning to go to this extreme you are likely not going to ever max this out.

In order to find the size of your current image, you need to click on image and then click on Image Size.

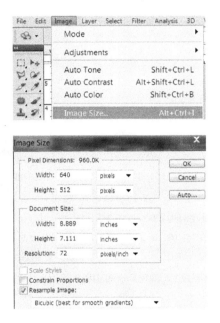

This area will tell you how many pixels wide and how many pixels high your image is, but it will also give you some other information such as the document width and height along with the resolution size. These are for printing and for web development purposes as web developer need to know how to scale the image to phone size. Without knowing the resolution of a picture, it becomes very difficult to correctly set the size of a word or picture on a phone.

Introduction to the Toolbar

What does the first line of the Tool bar do?

The first line inside of the Tool bar is all about selecting an area, which means you will be visiting this area very often. This includes invisible selections, which allow you to just select an area much like you would inside of Paint from Microsoft with a little bit more control, positional selections, which are great for an artist's eye to pick out where they need to curb the corner a little bit and other great options like Vector graphics, and some cropping tools. We'll go over each one to make sure you understand it.

Marquee Tools

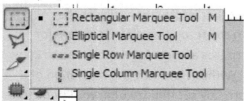

Marquee tools are for blank selections, such as moving boxes or circles around the area. These are not tools that you use when you are trying to remove a pimple from the face, but rather a description box on a web page. They have their uses, but I've found that they are really only good when modifying some type of document.

Move Tool

One you have selected a layer... let me repeat that, once you have selected *a layer* then you can use the move tool in order to move your selection around. The reason that I point out this difference is because some novices will become frustrated when they highlight a selection and wonder why only the selection box is moving and nothing else. You have to select the layer you want to move, or the element such as a cut layer or a text box layer.

Lasso Tools

The lasso tool is by far my most favorite type of selection tool because it gives you a lot of versatility. The regular lasso tool is used by physically circling the area you want to highlight.

The Polygonal Lasso Tool is a little different as it uses straight lines to do the same thing. Lastly, the Magnetic Lasso tool magnetically follows where you go and finds the deepest contrast in the nearest image to choose where its selection line will go. As you can tell, these selection tools are definitely useful when it comes to making minute selections.

Quick Selection Tools

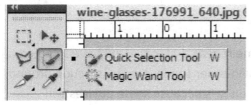

These are basically the same tools but with different implementations. The Quick Selection Tool is a blanker one-click magic wand tool. The Magic Wand Tool attempts to figure out what you want to select based on where you drag your cursor.

Slice Tools

The slice tools are really different from each other and I really don't know why they are put together like this. Crop allows you to select an area you want to separate from the rest of the picture to keep. Slice, on the other hand, is a famous tool amongst those who develop websites because you use the slice tool when you go to save. You are marking out different images that you want to save separately so that you can place them on a website. This does not become apparent until it is too frustrating to understand and then a quick Google search causes a little more frustration until you finally wind up on a final answer.

When you use the slice tool, you mark out areas you want to save, like this.

Once you have marked these areas out, you need to click on File and then click on Save for Web and Devices

Save	Ctrl+S
Save As...	Shift+Ctrl+S
Check In...	
Save for Web & Devices...	Alt+Shift+Ctrl+S
Revert	F12

This will bring you to a screen that looks confusing at first, but you don't really need to do much here except choose a preset up the right hand corner as we've talked about before, before hitting the save button. This will open up the folder locater where you can choose to save your images as separate sliced pieces of the same pie.

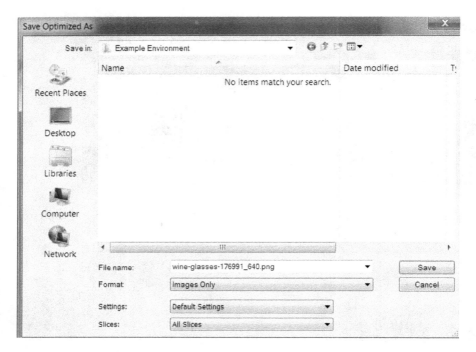

Once you hit save here, the image will be divided into slices, which for me looks like this

| wine-glasses-176 | wine-glasses-176 | wine-glasses-176 | wine-glasses-176 |
| 991_640_01.png | 991_640_02.png | 991_640_03.png | 991_640_04.png |

As you can see, just like it mentioned with the slices I have four different pieces because of how I chose to slice my image. This is why it is great for document and web designers who need to slice up an art image into different bits to lay out on a web document.

Misc Tools

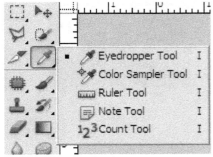

I won't be showing how to use these tools because they are pretty self-explanatory. The only one I will show you how to use is the ruler tool because this is different that almost all the others.

The Most Common Manipulation Technique Used With These Tools

Background Replace

By far the most common reason to use any of these tools is to remove the background. As an example, I have used the eyedropper tool in combination with an advanced feature called Color Range in the Select Menu to select the green of the background and remove it. Below are the before and after pictures.

Toolbar Part 2

What does the second line of the Toolbar do?

The second line of the Toolbar would be the "fix it" category as there are a lot of options to repair a picture here. This area is highly used by those who manipulate photos because most individuals who manipulate photos are often seeking to making them look smooth sleek, and not overly sharpened. This area allows for me to blur nastily sharpened areas, patch up holes that may have been deleted, and even use other pieces of skin to cover up a blemish. I tend to stay in this area of the toolbar the most.

Patching Tools

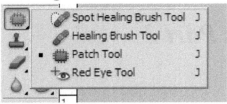

The Patching Tools are really for repair complexion. I've never seen these tools for much else beyond repeat patterns that already exist there. For example, if you needed to remove a hair and this left a big wide streak of transparency that you needed to fill in then you would use the Spot Healing Brush Tool in Combination with the Clone Stamp Tool.

Brush Tools

The Brush tools tend to be for touch up work. Using the previous example, we can assume that there was some shade where that piece of hair was and, since we removed the hair, that piece of hair is no longer there. We can now use a shader brush on the skin we duplicated to provide some shadows to that area. The brush area are primarily for artists who use Photoshop to do their artwork rather than photo manipulation. I will say that you can make a rather nice shade with a large, high opacity brush if the picture is a tad too bright though.

Clone Tools

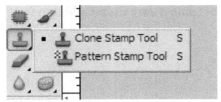

The clone tools are the same tool taking from different locations. The Clone Stamp clones one area on to another area via position. This can be problematic if you intend to clone a large area as you will run into areas you didn't want to clone if you don't position your source correctly. The Pattern Stamp Tool is something I have never found to be useful, but it allows you to paint on a preset pattern on to the image. I suppose this might be useful in map creation, but I haven't seen a potential use for it anywhere else.

The Clone Stamp is extremely useful in my case as I tend to make minute mistakes in my work and prefer to repair them as I go along. As an example, I see something wrong in the glasses we manipulated before.

Let's see if I can take the pattern tool and fool someone into thinking it was originally part of that glass.

As you can see, I took the image material from one of the other glasses and cloned it on to the repair site. This tool as become a very useful addition to my manipulation arsenal.

History Brush

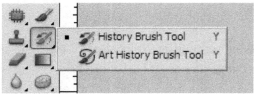

The art history brush is really useful if you want to reverse what you did in a specific place. I've rarely used this as part of image manipulation, but it is great to have if you don't have the material to patch from or you cannot clone it from some other location.

Eraser Tools

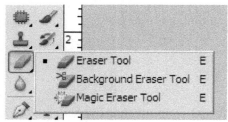

These are in every program, as you will always need to erase something in a program. Having said that, I've never had to go beyond the basic eraser even though Photoshop offers some potentially handy alternatives. The Background Eraser tool erases the data in the layers above the layer you currently have selected. This is useful if you want to cut via layer and then use more of a precision-based tactic to remove the background as we did earlier.

Wide-Area Paint Tools

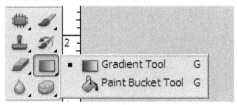

These are quite obvious in what they do. One paints an entire area with a specific color while the other applies a gradient to your image in the direction you click and drag. These are wider area paints, which means I've never had to actually use them. In fact, in my decade of using Photoshop I have never seen a single person use either one of these tools.

Art Style Tools Part 1 and 2

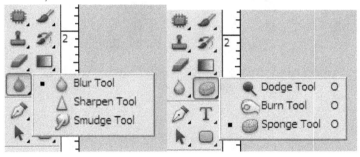

These are my **favorite** tools of Photoshop, beyond Liquefy and Perspective Point. The first three, blur, sharpen, and smudge are very obvious. Burn should also be obvious, but sponge and dodge definitely are not. Let's cover sponge because it is actually really useful. The sponge provides either more color or less color, otherwise known as saturation or desaturation. The dodge tool and burn tool are opposites of each other where the burn tool brings forth darkness, the dodge tool will bring forth light. These are old camera exposure techniques from before we did everything digitally and physical manipulation was the only way. I'm going to show you how you can use smudge and blur to fix the jagged edges our previous cut forced the cups into. Right now, it looks like this:

However, after I apply smudge and when I finally apply blur, the final product looks like:

This is why I tend to use these tools in a combo rather than using them separately.

Finishing Up The Toolbar

What does the third line of the Toolbar do?

The third line of the tool bar is primarily for text tools and vector art. Needless to say, we won't be going over much in this area.

Pen and Anchor Tools

If you can master these, you will have mastered the most accurate and advanced form of selection in Photoshop. I don't really use these that much unless I need the cut to be pinpoint exact. The reason being is that even though this is the most accurate, it is also the most time consuming and really doesn't offer much of a benefit except in some very few and rare occasions. An example of when I might use these tools is if I am trying to cut out the shape of a product or a sword, then I would use this but otherwise I would just use Quick Selection and mess around with the plus an minuses.

Text Tools

I tend to use text tools when I plan to put a title text into the photo. As an example, I might decide that I want the text of a specific thumbnail to arch above the subject with the text "The More You Know." I would select my text tool and the head all the way to the right of the image at the top in the Current Action bar to click on Warp Text. Warp Text will allow be to preselect the arch and then I can bend it to what I think looks correct.

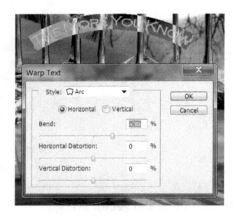

However, I can also click on the 3D option Repousse underneath 3D and select Text Layer.

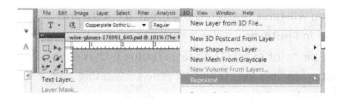

This will bring up the 3D options and you will not only see my final result, but also why 3D requires an entirely separate book to go over all the different aspects.

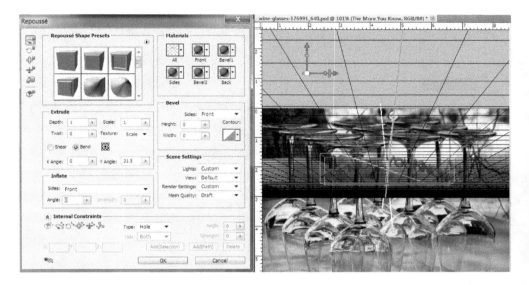

Path and Direction Tools

The Path and Direction Tools relate to the Pen and Anchor tools. Path allows you to control where the path is located on your image whereas the Direction Tool allows you to control the individual anchors within a path. This usually goes unnoticed by the novice for a while as they just need to click on the Path in Paths for these tools to auto-activate. In my opinion, their existence is rather redundant because of this and I think it should just be an auto-activate in newer versions.

Shape Tools

Shape Tools will make you feel like you are in Microsoft Paint once again, or a similar basic painting program, as these are just basic shapes. I've never really used these in professional projects and I just prefer to draw my material out. However, if you want to use this tool then who am I to tell you no.

What does the last line of the Toolbar do?

Welcome to the last part of the Toolbar and this section will be another brief section since most of these are simply too complex to cover in this one book. This section main controls color and perspective. The first too controls the 3D objects and their cameras, which is the part we will skip. Then we have Window Pane Adjustment Tools of which the hand allows you to move the picture up, down, left, and right in accordance to your view and the other hand allows you to rotate the image, but I prefer to just use image rotate when I go to rotate an image. I can see how the latter would be very useful if you were drawing rather than editing. Likewise, we have the zoom tool, which I just press Alt on my keyboard and roll the mouse back and forth to zoom.

Finally, we have the color selection tool. Now, as I mentioned before, the color tab on the right hand side can determine what color the box is but understand which box means what is vital. You need to look at the top left box as the pencil head and the bottom right box as the pencil eraser. If the top left is black and the bottom right is green, then when you paint something it will be black but when you erase something, it will be green.

Now, if you click on that top left box, you will get the option to see the Color Picker, which has a number of wonderful options. As a web developer, I tend to only care about colors recognized by the web, but you may be different. Once you select a color from here you can select "Ok" but you can also add that color to your swatches for later use. Now, if you want a collage of scheme colors or colors that complement each other then I suggest you check out the Color Libraries option.

On the very top, you have something called book, which should really say "presets" but they're trying to go for the authentic feeling of choosing a painting scheme from color pallets This is where you can use the presets to do any normal color selection you would have wanted to do on your own.

Welcome to Adjustments!

You have finally begun to reach the end of the book, but you're probably like "I thought we were going to do some manipulation?" Well, you would be correct but we had to get to the part where we could do those manipulations and now that we're at adjustments, we can finally get into some adjustments. We're going to spend our time transforming this:

Into something else.

What does the first line of Adjustments do?

The first line of Adjustments adjusts the level of brightness in a picture along with how much data we want to retain in the picture. This may not make sense, but if you remember my explanation about lack of quality often meant lack of data then you can see what I mean when I say that sometimes you can achieve a rustic feel in a photo by losing data.

Brightness/Contrast

The first one we are going to manipulate is Brightness/Contrast. Brightness just determines whether the picture is dark or light. Contrast is where you can determine how much color is inside of a photograph. For this one, we will be lower the brightness so that it seems like more of an even photograph and we will up the contrast to give it a more bold look.

Levels

The levels control the lows, mids, and highs of a photograph. This really just means that it controls the shadows, the colors, and then the lack of colors in a photograph. It's not too difficult to grasp, but you have to mess with levels in order to do so.

In this one, we're going to up the levels in the shade while also lowering the levels of the non-colors so that we can achieve an even darker feel.

Curves

Curves also represent the lows, mids, and highs of a photograph. This is a graphical form of what we see in in levels, but now we're going to do something a little different. We're going to use a selection tool to grab the ground that the bike is standing on and make it much darker. Once again, I plan on using the Color Range and Eye Dropper combination I made before. Then I will go ahead and delete this, which will make it look like this:

However, we can very well leave our bike on the road so let's go grab a road and some grass, maybe even both in one photo but I doubt it.

This one looks good, but it doesn't match out perspective, so let's see if we can bring it in and angle it into our perspective. Therefore, to bring it in, we just drag it over to our picture. This will produce little sizing boxing we can use to size the image.

However, the picture has way too much color for me to know whether I am positioning it in the right way so I can lower that by making sure I have that layer highlight and then lowering the Opacity in the top right corner of the layer box.

Now that I can see what I am doing, I can now see if I need to shrink or blow up the photo, which I have concluded I need to blow up.

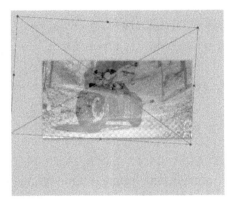

I have also concluded that I need to change the perspective, so if I right click on the image I can choose perspective.

I can also choose to skew the image by selecting skew from the same menu. Finally, this is the result that I get.

However, as you can see, we're not quite done yet as we need to replace the background from the old photo and crop out the transparency cause by the distortion. Let's drag that background layer down below the motorcycle.

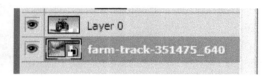

In order to remove that background, I'm going to choose the regular eraser and begin erasing *after* I have selected the motorcycle. However, I'm just going to do this until I can only see mostly blue, from which I will then use another eyedropper and Color Range Combo to remove the remaining blue. First, I will select the eyedropper and use it on the light blue. Then I will go up to Select and then Color Range.

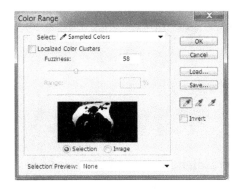

Now what you see here is an image that has been turned into black and white and you are trying to get all the color you want to select to be white while keep the remaining material as dark as possible. You can adjust the colors by choosing "fuzziness," going back and forth between values. Once you think you are satisfied, then you can click delete. This got me this result so far.

We are still not done as we need to get rid of the remainder, crop out the transparency, and we still don't have that nighttime feel. So, let's do everything except the nighttime feel and this is the result of my effort.

Ah and now, we have a new problem. The resolution of the background does not match the resolution of the subject. This means that we need to lose data in the subject. We can fix this by having and enormous low strength blur on the subject. This is what I got, but I also shrunk the subject as the subject is simply too big for the photo to be realistic. To select the subject, you must press control and then select the image next to the layer name. This is my result.

Still not done though because the forest background is actually under the influence of our motorcycle's effects, so we need to remove those if we are to properly edit them. Just drag the forest background up to the top layer of the layers. However, this will prevent us from seeing the bike, but that's okay and easily fixable. Now you just need to reselect the bike, make sure the forest background is highlight, and delete the bike. The selection lines will prevent you from deleting anything outside of the lines and by selecting the bike we can make a perfect fit hole for the bike to be seen through. Here is my result.

Now it's on to fix this bad boy to the proper resolution.

Exposure

Exposure is another lighting effect and it is meant to symbolize the exposure we see that is similar to a camera. However, since what we need is something that lowers resolution we are not going to be using this tool for this photo.

Adjustments Part 2

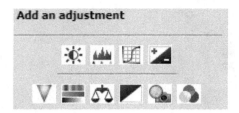

What does the second line of Adjustments do?

The second line of Adjustments controls the color balances of the entire picture so while the first one may have been able to control the light, this next one is able to control the overall color of the picture. We won't be adding anything more into this picture until the last section of this book where we can find a gradient map.

Vibrance

Vibrance is often how bright the colors are and how high of a hue is in those colors. This means it will take your highlights from the layer you have selected and increase all colors past a certain threshold.

Hue/Saturation

Hue and Saturation are a little different from the previous one as Hue controls the color of the object, Saturation controls the strength of those colors, and there's a last option of lightness, which also controls the lightness of those colors.

Color Balance

Color Balance is another method of controlling the shadows, mids, and highs of a photo. However, in addition to controlling those colors this option also give you control over the different spectrum of colors. This makes a rather big impact when you are looking to make sure that a certain color, like your rustic red, takes prominence over other colors. I use this option the most whenever I find that the photographs I am editing are comprised of somewhat dull colored imagery. Having the control over those colors allows me to breathe life back into the photo.

Black and White

The next couple of adjustments are also filters, which mean not only do they change the color of a subject but they also change the theme of the subject. This one alters the imagery so that it is in black and white, which means when you go to control the colors you are really just controlling the different shades there are of black and white. This adjustment fits a niche market of artists and it is very useful to have a color-editing program also be able to handle old-style photography because that is rare nowadays.

Photo Filter

The photo filter is more of an auto-correction for old lenses. You may have an old camera that tends to bring that incandescent glow with it into the photo. However, many, like myself, dislike it when old technology force changes on to photographs that should not have been changed. Moreover, sometimes the camera doesn't catch the proper light in the environment. That is what this adjustment is for and it does a very good job at correcting these issues.

Channel Mixer

The channel mixer is the end all be all of color editors with the ability to change colors in every channel. By channel, we are talking about RGB and alpha. Alpha is the channel that controls opacity.

Adjustments Part 3

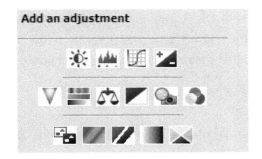

What does the last line of Adjustments do?

The last line of Adjustments are "effects" in the most basic sense of the term. These adjustments allow you to change the balance of colors, the contrast of colors, the resolution of colors, and even the removal of entire colors. I don't use much in this category on a daily basis except for gradient map as it helps out with the balancing of resolutions.

Invert

Inverting is kind of obvious as to what it does: it inverts the color of the selected object. What you likely didn't know is that when you are trying to "magic" select something or, better yet, color range select something it can make a huge difference when you are trying to grab hair. The change in color can often allow the hair to become darker while the environment around it becomes lighter. This makes it much easier to grab hair and make sure it isn't cut out from the picture.

257

Posturize

Posturize is the effect you get from making old posters, but since we have better material you could call this retro poster making. Most art programs offer this because it was a unique style that almost faded away with the passage of technology.

Threshold

Threshold is another black and white effect, but it is much simpler than the Black and White of the second line. You just get to choose the threshold of allowable color.

Gradient Map

All right, so now we are in gradient mapping and we're going to do to kinds of gradient design here. First, we need to create a noise gradient by hand in order to lower the overall resolution of the bike. Then we need to create a gradient that allows for the mixture of the colors from the background with the colors of the foreground. First, create a new layer and place it above the motorcycle. You can do this by going to Layer and then New and then click on Layer and just press OK when the text dialog pops up. You should now have another layer that you can position above the motorcycle. Now you need to click on the forestland eyeball next to its layer. This will make that invisible to us for the time being. Finally, choose the fill bucket from the Toolbar and choose black, and then fill in the new layer. You should now have a black layer with nothing visible. We will now go up to Filter and Choose Noise, from which we will Add Noise to the layer.

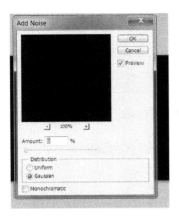

A nice Gaussian of strength six should do us just fine for adjusting the resolution. Now it is time to turn down the opacity to twenty-one percent, but I think we should cover the background in that darkness so that the lighting seems more realistic so go ahead and change the layout of your layers to this.

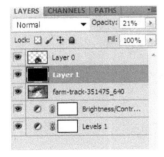

Now we're going to add a gradient to the motorcycle to make it look a little more rugged, so right click on the motorcycle, and choose blending options. Now you can choose the gradient overlay from the menu. In here, you should input these parameters.

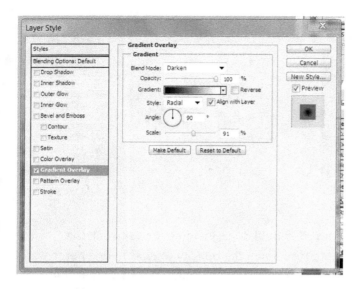

All right, now we should have a very nice looking rustic bike like this one.

The blending options allow for a much singular control over an image, but just messing around with the options in here should be enough to figure it out. Darken takes the current colors and darkens them whereas multiply takes the shade you choose and multiplies them in your image. Overlays just place the colors on top. Now we need to merge all of these together and use our final gradient.

In order to merge all the elements of a photo together, you must highlight them all, right-click, and then choose Merge Layers.

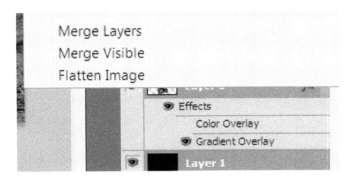

Now you can choose the gradient tool from the Wide-Area Tools where the fill tool is. In the Current Action Bar, there is a color, a light direction, a Mode, and an opacity. We are going to change the light direction to the first option. Then we are going to change the opacity to 10%. We will turn the Mode to Normal. Finally, we will direct the angle like so:

Now we are done modifying this picture and I'm sure you've learned a ton in the process if you managed to follow along.

Selective Color

Selective Color is another way of modifying all the colors at once and it is very similar to channel mixer only you have access to all the colors those channels would normally effect without effecting the channels. I know, confusing, but I'm sure someone finds it useful.

Conclusion

Welcome to the end! I hope you enjoyed yourself, I know I have. I am writing this at the end because I wanted to congratulate you on finishing your first picture to be edited in Photoshop. Well, maybe not really, but for some might this might hold true and I congratulate you all anyway. Here is the difference between the beginning picture and the end result.

It certainly has changed its looks and it may be rough around the edges, but we all have time to improve! Until next time.